Eternity in View

TIMOTHY S. WEAVER

Editing and content review by
Geri Weaver
Robert K. Weaver
Cheryl K. Weaver
Beth Medeiros

ISBN 978-1-0980-1157-4 (paperback)
ISBN 978-1-0980-1158-1 (digital)

Christian Faith Publishing, Inc.
832 Park Avenue
Meadville, PA 16335
www.christianfaithpublishing.com

Scripture quotations are from the ESV® Bible (The Holy Bible, English Standard Version®), copyright © 2001 by Crossway, a publishing ministry of Good News Publishers. Used by permission. All rights reserved.

Printed in the United States of America

PROLOGUE

Several years ago, a friend of mine informed me that she no longer considered herself a Christian. Despite her efforts to develop a relationship with Jesus, she was unable to feel any real connection and no longer believed that God was real. I don't know why God has revealed Himself to some in real and lasting ways while others are left searching, but I believe that in all of us there is a God-shaped hole that can only be filled by His presence. And unless we find Him, there will never be any real and lasting satisfaction and contentment.

This book is a testimony of how God has worked in the events of my life and how He has helped me to overcome tragedy and adapt to the new lifestyle that came out of it. I am blessed to have experienced God's presence in my life amidst my struggles, and through it all, I am convinced that God is real and in control of all things.

I do not believe that there is any such thing as coincidence. At the time God created the universe and everything in it, including the nature of time itself, He providentially knew each living thing intimately enough to know how it would respond to every imaginable combination of stimuli. Although interacting with and at times entering into His creation throughout history, God exists outside of time and space and can instantaneously see the entirety of His creation, including every event that has occurred in every place throughout all time. He can see the past, present, and future more clearly than we can see our current reality. He knows the thoughts and intentions of every heart and mind that He created, and understands how every possible decision and action would affect the world.

At the moment of creation, He knew every possible combination of the number of created beings, the place and time where each of these beings would exist, the natural phenomena that would exist at the time each would live, and the effect that the actions of each would have upon others. At that moment, He created the world according to His ultimate plan and purpose, intentionally choosing the place and time that each person would live. God granted individuals the freedom of choice to act according to each one's volition, but knowing the outcome of all decisions and actions in advance and using those results according to His plan.

Nothing happens that God does not explicitly and purposely allow. I believe that He allows suffering and pain in the lives of individuals to make Himself known and reveal Himself to the world. The very presence of suffering is a consequence of sin, which God allowed to manifest itself as a result of giving people the freedom of choice.

I believe that this world that we live in is only the beginning, that our present circumstances are only temporary, and that a greater eternal reality is yet to come that will render all that we are living through as trivial.

I want to thank my parents, who helped me to recount the details of my early life and the events surrounding my accident. I also thank my wife for supporting me in this effort.

I pray that you will enjoy reading my life story and that God's blessing will be upon you in your life.

Developing Interest
in Gymnastics

I WAS BORN IN Lancaster County and lived with my mother and father until age two. Shortly after my brother was born, my parents divorced. For a short time after my grandmother died, my mother, with my brother and me, moved in with my grandfather. He soon remarried, and we found another place to live. For several years when I was young, my mother worked full-time. We enjoyed the time with my grandparents while she was at work. We frequently spent time with them after school and occasionally walked to their house where my mother picked us up later. My grandparents were significant influences in my life at that time. When I was nine years old, my mother met a gentleman who attended our church. They were married the following year, and my new father formally adopted my brother and me as his children. We relocated from Mountville to New Holland, Pennsylvania, and began a new life.

While living in Mountville, I developed an interest in gymnastics. The elementary school I attended had a lot of gymnastics equipment, and I thoroughly enjoyed doing gymnastics in gym class. In fourth grade, I enjoyed watching an older student swing between the parallel bars and push himself up, over one of the bars, and off the side for a dismount. At recess, I observed other students: a boy who frequently walked around on his hands and a girl doing handsprings. I spent hours balancing on my hands for as long as I could and attempting to walk as far as possible without falling. My efforts did not always end well. Once while walking around the living room, I fell into the TV and broke the power knob. TVs at that time did not have remote controls, and from that point on, the TV required needle-nose pliers to turn on and off or adjust the volume. Every year, the fifth and sixth grade students presented a gymnastics show for the school. Although only in fourth grade, I performed a floor routine with skills I had learned in gym class. It was my first gymnastics routine. I was unaware at the time, but that was only the beginning, with many more yet to come.

As a family, we visited a gymnastics camp in Woodward, Pennsylvania. This event helped to spark my interest in competitive gymnastics. After my parents were married, I was thrilled to learn that there was a gym in New Holland and that I would be able to take classes.

When my parents took me to register, I watched a boy around my age swinging to a handstand on the parallel bars. Before long, we would be teammates and friends.

That year, I also remember watching gymnastics in the 1984 Olympics and trying to imitate things that I had seen performed by the athletes. I spent hours trying to learn a press handstand from a seated position. Eventually, I succeeded and went to my instructor and soon-to-be-coach Larry and said, "Watch this."

A couple of months after beginning classes, Larry presented me with an opportunity to join the prep team. I committed to practicing two nights a week, instead of just one, and would be able to learn routines and begin to compete. I now recognize the commitment that my parents had made and wonder if they realized at that time the magnitude of the decision at hand. I am immensely thankful for all they did for me over the years following that initial investment.

The week before joining the team, I had attended the Friday night football game at Garden Spot High School. It was a fun evening and I thought these games might become a regular hangout. Following that night, however, I rarely made it back, soon finding myself in the gym between twelve and fifteen hours per week. These and other sacrifices were ones I was more than willing to make.

As a ten-year-old, I began competing as a class IV gymnast, based mostly on my age. Age and skill level determined placement from class VI to class I, and eventually the elite level for the most experienced gymnasts. That first year, I easily qualified to compete at state championships. With a couple of months remaining before states, I began to learn the class III routines. At the year's final state qualifier, I had the opportunity to compete as a class III, a challenge I eagerly embraced and proceeded to qualify for states that first year at a class III as well as IV level. I opted to compete as a class III at states, where I qualified for and went on to compete at the regional competition.

It was clear that God had given me a natural ability in gymnastics, and I was excited about where it might take me. I wondered if I might someday compete in the Olympics.

Gymnastics, Education, Family, and Fun

Many of the experiences I had during the next five years were unrelated, but all my memories during that time began to prepare me for bigger things to come. Although I was unaware of it happening, a support network was developing around me, which would be vital during the following stage of my life.

While I was still living in Mountville, I was always involved in sports of some kind. I played little league baseball for a couple of years and basketball for a season but struggled in both. I liked and did well in soccer. I probably would have continued in soccer had I not found my way into gymnastics. But once I got started in gymnastics, I had little interest in anything else. I took saxophone lessons for a short time but quickly decided that I didn't have time for it, especially during the school year. Maybe it was an excuse because I didn't want to practice, but the amount of time I spent in the gym seemed to justify my decision nonetheless. Even though I hate quitting anything, gymnastics was taking top priority over everything else.

That first year in gymnastics, as I quickly progressed and improved, was like a whirlwind sweeping me along, and I loved every minute of it.

Over the next five years the schedule of my gymnastics practices and competitions primarily determined the direction of my life. What I remember of that time, especially during the school year, was going to school, doing my homework, eating, sleeping, and spending as much time in the gym as possible. Our scheduled practices were between two and three hours long, and I was consistently in the gym between twelve and fifteen hours each week.

I grew up going to church on Sundays and went to youth group on Wednesday evenings. Competitions were mostly on weekends and frequently on Sundays. There were many occasions that I took my gymnastics attire and equipment to church, after which we changed and headed straight to a competition. Other weeks we did not make it to church at all. I feel like I was able to have a developing relationship with Jesus during that time, but I have to admit that my primary focus during those years was gymnastics. Still, God was developing a foundation in my life on which a lot of trials would later pile. I developed an interest in Christian apologetics—the defense of the faith—and learned early in my life that the entire Bible is true and trustworthy and able to stand up to scrutiny and critical analysis. I believed firmly in the inerrancy of Scripture, salvation through Christ alone, and that all things happen according to God's divine plan and knowledge of things to come.

We attended Calvary Church my whole life, and I used to joke that I began attending Calvary nine months before I was born. The church grew quite a bit during that time, and my faith was also developing. Growing up in the church, I had many friends in the youth group. Although I had a couple of good friends, I didn't develop many close friendships.

My relationships with peers at school were not much different. I got along with and related to just about everybody to one degree or another. I had many acquaintances, but few, if any, were more than surface relationships. That's not to say that I didn't have genuine friends who cared for and about me and I them, but I rarely let anyone get too close. Because of this, I have little significant contact with most of my peers from that time in my life and find now that I have little in common with most of them.

I enjoyed school and was motivated to do my best. I always planned to go to college and tried to make my academic schedule difficult. I took as many advanced placement (AP) classes as possible, thinking that if I was capable of doing the work, I should. To do otherwise would be second best.

I was always interested in art and thought that I might choose an art-related career. I was not the best artist in the school by any stretch of the imagination, but did enjoy it and did pretty well. My creations were usually a little unordinary, and I liked to stretch my imagination. One project I still have sitting on my desk at work is a whistle I made out of clay. We fashioned clay whistles; mine formed into the head of a flamingo, glazed white with black spots, and dubbed a flaming-cow (pronounced similar to flamingo).

I spent many hours drawing with paper, pens, and pencils, but that aspect of my life has mostly disappeared over the years. My creativity, however, has emerged in other ways as I have needed, on numerous occasions, to find unique solutions to life's problems.

Throughout elementary school, junior high, and high school, I also enjoyed expressing myself through dance. I listened to pop, R&B, and rap music and enjoyed imitating and practicing the dance steps and routines popularized by many performers. (I would have loved having YouTube back then!) For a short time, I also delved into break dancing and hip-hop, with an occasional backflip and other skills I learned in the gym. I enjoyed going to school dances and, when able, teen dance clubs. I also tried writing and performing rap music, but more for personal enjoyment than public display.

In gymnastics, my teammates soon became my second family and the gym my home away from home. My parents dropped me off just about every weekday evening and Saturday morning and picked me up a few hours later. Gymnastics had quickly become the most significant part of my life. When I first started gymnastics, a New Holland industrial park warehouse housed the gym. Less than two years after I began, a devastating fire burned the warehouse, the gym, and everything in it to the ground. Unable to comprehend the future of the gym at that time, I wondered if I would ever do gymnastics again. But the gym soon reopened in a temporary location, a small building in the heart of New Holland. During that time, we also visited other gyms to use their equipment, especially their floor exercise areas, as we prepared for competitions. At our temporary facility, we did not have a full-size floor exercise area, just a tumble strip, making it difficult to do full routines. Eventually, however, we moved into a new facility where the gym resides to this day.

During each competition season, we worked with our coaches to develop our routines. Each season consisted of eight to fifteen meets in which we executed two different routines. Compulsory routines designed by the United States Gymnastics Federation (USGF) differed according to class, but everybody within each class did the same skills. Scoring was dependent on who did the skills most cleanly and with the best execution. Coaches worked with each gymnast to develop optional routines to showcase what each gymnast could do on an individual level. The season always began with competitions in which we performed strictly compulsory routines. Later in the year, the format shifted to include optionals as well. Some events were one or the other, and in some, we competed both.

Competitions were frequent, and we saw consistent, repeated competition with gyms each season. Members and coaches of other teams, as well as the judges, became a sort of extended family.

I was accustomed to being on the podium after each competition and enjoyed the recognition. My accolades were building, and I was becoming known among my peers as one of the best.

During those years we did a lot of traveling within our region, consisting of Pennsylvania, Maryland, Delaware, New York, New Jersey, Virginia, and West Virginia, and became accustomed to spending nights in hotels. Sometimes we traveled with our families. At other times we went as a team in our coach Larry's van, no seats or seat belts, just a big open carpeted van into which we all piled. As you can probably guess, regulations were a lot less strict than they are now. The first year I went to nationals, held in Oshkosh, Wisconsin, was more for the experience than having any expectation of winning, and we traveled without families. It was just me, my teammate Keith, and our two coaches for the only time I ever needed airfare to travel to a competition.

Summertime afforded more time to spend on other activities, and I enjoyed swimming, biking, skateboarding, street hockey, fishing, video games, and other recreational activities that varied from year to year. One Christmas, my brother and I received freestyle bikes as gifts, and we enjoyed doing tricks. One trick that I could do well was surfing, in which I coasted, standing straight up with one foot on the seat and one on the handlebars to steer. My brother had more time for biking than I did and was much better than I was. I always enjoyed watching him on his bike.

Each summer, my family would spend a week or two at the beach. My brother and I spent at least one, sometimes two weeks at various church camps, and most summers I also spent an additional week at a gymnastics camp with my teammates.

Triumph and Trouble

I N THE FALL of 1989, I began my sixth year of competitive gymnastics. After qualifying for nationals the previous year, I was excited to try to better my performance over the new season. Some of my teammates were in my same grade in school, but the date of my birthday left me in the 13–15 age group for one year longer before advancing. While my teammates advanced to the 16–18 class I level, it suited me to compete again as a class II for one more year. I would be one of the older and more experienced in my age group and class, and I hoped that this would give me a better chance to do well at nationals. Optional routines would be the same either way.

In January 1990, I was sick with the flu for the week leading up to our first two optional meets of the year. As a result, I did not have an opportunity to finalize the development of my routines. As we approached the weekend, we decided that my health had improved enough for me to try competing—one competition on Saturday and one on Sunday. My coach and I adjusted my routines so that I could comfortably execute, and I did my best. Sunday night, I finished the weekend with two first-place all-around awards.

That weekend took its toll on my body. Feeling not at all well on Tuesday evening at the gym, I didn't do much but sit and watch. After practice, I went home and went to bed. The next thing I remember is waking up in the hospital three days later.

On Wednesday morning, my family was unable to wake me up. They took me, in a comatose state, to the doctor, who sent them immediately to the emergency room. I had contracted a viral form of encephalitis. The doctors were uncertain at first if the infection was viral or bacterial, nor could they give my parents any assurance that I would ever revive. They prescribed a broad range of antibiotics, but they warned my parents that should I awake, I might have brain damage, be blind, or be confined to a wheelchair for the rest of my life.

Three days later, I woke up. Aside from being in the hospital in a weakened state, I don't recall feeling any significant effects from the illness. Within a couple of weeks, following therapy and doctor visits, I returned to school and the gym and resumed my endeavor toward a return trip to nationals. God had brought my family through a scary ordeal, but He is good, and things were moving in a positive direction once again. As the season progressed, I continued to balance gymnastics, school, church, and family life. I continued to do well in school. I turned sixteen during that year, got my driver's permit, and began to learn to drive.

As I had done every year since beginning gymnastics, I qualified for the state and regional competitions. Regional championships that year were at William and Mary College. At that competition, I performed my most complete set of routines from the entire season. The one big exception was my optional pommel horse routine, which was awful, but not entirely unexpected. Rings and pommel horse were my two weakest events, with pommel horse a clear worst. Although I spent a lot of time practicing those routines, I think I lacked the upper body strength necessary to excel in those disciplines. Still, my skill level was increasing and my execution more consistent as we got closer to a return trip to nationals. At regionals, I finished seventh in the all-around competition, qualifying me to the position of alternate on the region 7 team for the national championships.

Over the years that I had competed, our travels to different parts of the region gave us the added opportunity for sightseeing at various tourist attractions. The prior year, regionals took place in upstate New York. While there, we took the time to cross into Canada and visit Niagara Falls. This year, in Williamsburg, Virginia, we spent time touring Colonial Williamsburg. We also spent a day at Busch Gardens that week. We enjoyed the amusement park, which seemed practically empty with school still in session. I think my brother and I each rode the Loch Ness Monster and Big Bad Wolf roller coasters about twenty times each, just running round and round to keep getting on again and again.

After school had ended for the year, I got my first job over the summer. I worked as a dishwasher at Plain & Fancy, a local Lancaster County restaurant. It was hard work, but it gave me the opportunity to earn some money and get driving practice to and from work.

The weekend of nationals was quickly approaching. I don't remember if I felt prepared, but I know that a lot of hard work went into getting my routines ready for competition. That year, nationals was in Baltimore, Maryland, not more than a couple of hours drive from our home. Being that close meant my family would be in the stands watching and cheering for me. We were also planning a trip to the beach and were all packed and ready to leave from Baltimore immediately following the competition.

The championship began with an introduction of all the gymnasts and judges. When the announcer called my name, I walked out onto the floor, excited about the experience and proud to be wearing the region 7 team uniform, even though only as an alternate. Regardless of the eventual outcome at nationals, I was proud of myself and of what I had accomplished thus far that year.

During the competition, nothing about my routines was highly memorable, with one exception. My best event was always the horizontal bar. I enjoyed just swinging around and around the bar and letting my body fly. I had high expectations for myself on this event and was hoping to finish in the top ten. I performed my compulsory routine well on the first day of the championships. I was hopeful that a good performance in the optional session would move me into the top ten to compete in the high bar finals the next day.

My routine began well. I let go and successfully regrabbed the bar for my release skill. Nearly complete with only the dismount remaining, I swung around the bar twice and let go. As I let go, I heard the bar twang, the vibration indicating that I let go too early. Instead of rising to get the needed height to complete my full-twisting double-back dismount, I flew out and away and barely had enough height and time to complete the rotation. My feet hit the ground, my hands hit the ground, and I rolled out. That was it. I would most likely not qualify for finals.

I settled for fifteenth place but was happy to have done that well. Looking back, I know that fifteenth in the nation in anything is something to be proud of, but at the time, it was hard not to think that I could have done better. I left that competition telling myself, my coach, my dad, and anyone else, "There's always next year." I would be a class I the following year, and competition would be more difficult, but I was looking forward to the challenge. And so we left for a couple of weeks at the beach and some time away to relax before going back to the gym to prepare for the next year.

The Accident

WHEN WE RETURNED home from the beach, I was anxious to get back into the gym. I was now a class I and would have new routines to learn for the upcoming year. The last week in July, our team attended a gymnastics camp in Allentown, Pennsylvania. These trips were always refreshing because they enabled us to see ourselves from the perspective of different coaches and practice methods. We frequently got ideas for new skills to work on and stretched ourselves to new limits. During that week, I learned to do a full-twisting double-front flip off a mini trampoline into a pit of foam. I was excited about continuing to practice it back in our gym.

The following week, I was dropped off at the gym on Tuesday evening for practice. It was the first day back in our gym. Customarily, I and Keith, one of my teammates, came early, neither of our coaches having yet arrived.

Typically we would talk, stretch, or do some relaxed warm-up exercises. On that night, however, I allowed the excitement of the prior week to guide me. I set up the mini tramp and began to flip. After one or two flips, I tried the full-twisting double-front I had learned the previous week. I don't recall if my first attempt was completed successfully or with difficulty, but I tried again. This time, however, I became disoriented in the air, opened up out of my tuck too early, and dove head first into the pit. I passed through the looser foam blocks toward the surface that would have cushioned my fall had I landed in almost any other way. But head first, I hit the compacted foam near the bottom, near the concrete floor, six feet below floor level.

And there I stayed, upside down, unable to move and having difficulty breathing. Keith saw me fall and came in to assist. After moving enough foam to help me breathe, he stayed with me until the ambulance arrived. He tried comforting me, stating, "I'm sure it's only temporary." Oddly enough, I felt no pain of any kind, but I could not move a muscle.

My parents arrived shortly before the ambulance. I remember seeing my father looking down at me from the mat next to the pit. My parents were always there for me when I needed them, and this was no exception. The ambulance arrived, and the EMTs came into the pit. They fitted me with a brace to keep my head and neck immobilized, strapped me onto a stretcher, and lifted me out. Individually moving through the foam blocks was cumbersome, but before long, the EMTs successfully lifted me out. As they carried me to the ambulance, my coach Larry arrived and, in passing at the door, I just said, "hi."

The ambulance rushed me to the emergency room at Lancaster General Hospital (LGH). From that point on, the next few weeks are a blur of memories and images that I will try to relay as best I can. I soon learned that I had broken my neck, and, having broken a stabilizing piece off one of my vertebrae, I was very unstable.

Two screws fitted into the sides of my head and hooked to a weighted pulley system kept my neck stretched until going into surgery. I don't remember how soon after the accident I had surgery, but within a day or two of the accident, the fifth and sixth vertebrae in my neck were wired and fused together. After surgery, I wore a halo neck brace for the next couple of months until my neck bones had time to heal and solidify.

I emphasize here that the "bones" would heal. For those of you familiar with human anatomy and spinal cord injuries, you are well aware that there is more involved with neck and back injuries than healing bones. For the rest of you, the vertebrae that make up the spinal column are hollow in the center like a stack of washers. Through the center runs the spinal cord, which is the primary conduit of information traveling from the brain to all parts of the body. Neck and back injuries can result in partial or complete paralysis. This effect can be temporary or permanent depending on the severity of the injury and the trauma involved.

Pressure tests, temperature sensitivity tests, attempts at movement, and various other X-rays and evaluations were systematically and repeatedly undertaken to determine just how severe and long-lasting my injury might be. The doctors eventually concluded that my injury was complete, meaning that I had no functionality that would indicate that any brain signals were moving past the affected vertebrae in my neck. I would retain the use of my deltoid muscles in my shoulders and my biceps, and I would have some limited use of my wrists. Our brains control wrist flexors with signals emanating from the spinal cord at the C5 level. The focal point of the damage to my spine was at the C6 level. I would have no use of my triceps, which are controlled by signals emanating from the spinal cord at the C7 vertebrae below my injury. I would also have no use of my hands, which are controlled by signals between the C7 and T1 vertebrae. In effect, I could contract or bend my arms to lift things (although I could not grab them with my hands), but I could not straighten my arms to push away from me.

Understanding the full impact of what it meant to live as a quadriplegic would take time. While in the hospital, I was still hopeful that I would have a full recovery, although my current condition did not readily lend itself to an optimistic outlook. I couldn't move any part of my body below my armpits. My arms, as described above, were only partially usable, and I could not move my hands and fingers at all.

I also couldn't feel any external sensation below my armpits and on the majority of my arms. I had lost all control of my bodily functions and was barely able to feed myself. Feeding myself at all was dependent on what position I was in or what I was trying to eat, and most of the time I was forced to rely on others. Relying on others was difficult for me, as I was accustomed to being in control of my own body. My mind, however, was still fully intact, and this was a blow to my pride. I was a sixteen-year-old wearing a diaper and having to be completely taken care of by other people.

I don't recall if it was a direct result of the accident or something that happened after surgery, but at some point in the hospital, one of my lungs had collapsed. In the hospital, I also dealt with a lot of fluid in my lungs, and I contracted pneumonia. I had to have a tube periodically inserted through my nose and down my throat to evacuate the fluid. Doing my best to avoid this unpleasant experience, I intentionally and frequently tried to cough to clear my lungs as much as possible on my own. Because I no longer had use of my diaphragm, I had to have someone press on my stomach, in perfect timing with my breathing and cough attempts to give me a little extra air pressure to cough.

For a couple of days, I also required a respirator. At that time, I was not only unable to move and feel, but also unable to speak. Communication was difficult, as I could not write, and depending on my position, what limited use of my arms that I had was even more restricted. I remember using a card that was held by a parent, friend, or nurse. The card had the alphabet printed on it, and I was able to identify one letter at a time to slowly spell out what I wanted. Although I was able to communicate in this way, the process was slow and tedious and a real test of everyone's patience.

On one night in the hospital, I looked up at my parents and asked, "Is the room spinning or is it just me?" My temperature had risen to 106 degrees, and I was becoming delirious. The nurses promptly packed me with ice to cool my body.

Not long after surgery, I began occupational and physical therapy on a daily basis. While I was initially limited to stretching in bed, within a couple of weeks, my neck stabilized enough to transfer out of bed into a wheelchair, and I was able to leave my room. I would soon be ready to move to a more intensive rehabilitation hospital.

Personal Testing

DESPITE MY NEW physical limitations, I was still a sixteen-year-old teenager with a fully functional mind. I was completely aware of my present condition and circumstances. I remember thinking to myself while in the hospital, "My permit expires today," and wondered if I would ever be able to drive.

At this point, I had no understanding of the details and severity of my ongoing limitations. I remembered from years back when Mike King visited our church to tell his story. As a paraplegic, he had pushed his wheelchair from Anchorage, Alaska, to Washington, D.C. As I listened attentively to his story, I remember thinking that maybe I could handle being a para, but not a quad. Now I was being forced to see firsthand what it would be like to live as a quadriplegic, although at this point I was ignorant of what that meant. A quad, able to drive a van and live a significant part of his life independently, visited me at the hospital. Although I was encouraged by his visit, I still did not understand what exactly to expect. I was still too young in my injury to know what to ask him. The only thing on my mind that concerned me enough to ask was whether I would have no bowel control and have to wear diapers the rest of my life, something I was dealing with at the hospital at that time. He assured me that at rehab, I would work on training my body to work on a routine schedule and that these problems wouldn't be an ongoing concern. Other than that, I still naively believed that even if I could not walk, I could pull myself around with my hands and arms. I had also formulated a rope and pulley system to get to my existing bedroom on the second floor of our house. I hadn't yet come to the realization or acceptance that I would no longer have the balance, strength, or coordination to do such things. Being a quad, I would soon learn, would be much more limiting than anything that I could imagine at that time.

My trials also tested me spiritually. I knew from my upbringing that God is in control and that all things work together for good for those who love Him and are called according to His purpose (Romans 8:28). I had accepted Jesus as Lord and Savior at a young age, but my faith was being tested more at this time in my life than ever before. God showed me, through those who surrounded me in my time of need, that He is real and that He loves me.

My parents were my biggest supporters, and there was barely a time during the first few weeks after my accident that at least one of them wasn't there. We had a hard time convincing my mom to go home, and many nights she slept at the hospital. Much of my dad's time was spent researching and gathering information on quadriplegia and advocating on my behalf. He only worked half-time at his law practice while we dealt with the early stages of my disability. My brother stayed at a friend's house during this time.

While in the hospital, I was amazed at and thankful for the number of visitors, cards, and well wishes I received, and the many blessings that God poured my way. I had always tried to be friendly and peaceable with everyone I encountered, but the number of people who were impacted by my accident humbled me.

People I knew from church, school, and the gymnastics community visited me in the hospital. Some came from a great distance to encourage me, and it blessed me to have such support. Cards, flowers, balloons, and notes covered the walls in my hospital room. God gave me special favor with the hospital staff in allowing this, and I am eternally grateful for the care and attention I received while there. One nurse, Becky, became a close family friend for many years.

God also blessed me with a sense of peace about my inability to ever do gymnastics again. I was able to mentally and psychologically say goodbye to gymnastics and focus my attention on my recovery.

Should I have recovered, I am not sure that I would have returned to competitive gymnastics. While it was a tragic ending to my gymnastics career and my future was now unknown, I was never depressed or angry. I was content to leave my life and my future in God's hands and ready to embrace the new challenges that lay before me.

The doctors had me talk to a psychologist because they were sure that I should have been angry or depressed and was repressing my true feelings, but I was at peace with the whole process and trusted God in what He was allowing me to go through.

That's not to say that I never had moments of sadness or reflections of what I should have done differently, but I never forgot that God loved me, and I knew that I could trust Him because He is the author of my life and knows what He is doing.

Nevertheless, when I was injured, everything changed. I became acutely aware that I was not in control. A whole new unknown future lay before me. Within the first few months following my accident, I found this passage of Scripture that provided comfort that I have clung to since that time.

> Come now, you who say, "Today or tomorrow we will go into such and such a town and spend a year there and trade and make a profit"—yet you do not know what tomorrow will bring. What is your life? For you are a mist that appears for a little time and then vanishes. Instead you ought to say, "If the Lord wills, we will live and do this or that." (James 4:13–15, ESV)

God gave me a family that knew and loved God, and friends and a church who supported me in my time of need. As a child, I learned about God, how He worked in the past, and how Scripture points toward future prophetic fulfillment. God gave me an eternal perspective that encouraged me never to give up.

> What is your life? For you are a mist that appears for a little time and then vanishes. (James 4:14)

We were all made for eternity. While we all had a beginning at conception, our lives from that point on will have no end. Even if we would manage to live 150 years on earth, that amount of time is like a mist that quickly vanishes compared with the eternity for which we were created. While recognizing that time and eternity have no direct correlation, as eternity is outside time, I like to use the example of a yardstick to represent a comparison of time to eternity. Imagine a yardstick extending out with no end in either direction. Our time that we live on earth could be represented by a fraction of one of the measurement marks on the stick. When Keith, trying to comfort me (and probably himself) regarding my inability to move, told me immediately after I was injured, "I am sure it is only temporary," he was absolutely right! Although probably not what he meant, an eternal perspective has enabled me to endure knowing that *all* of life on earth is temporary, and we have yet to experience the awesome reality for which we were created.

The apostle Paul had the right perspective knowing that our sufferings are nothing compared with our eternal future glory.

> For I consider that the sufferings of this present time are not worth comparing with the glory that is to be revealed to us. (Romans 8:18)

He also recognized that all our accomplishments will pale in comparison to the glory that we will see with Christ for an eternity in heaven.

> But whatever gain I had, I counted as loss for the sake of Christ. Indeed, I count everything as loss because of the surpassing worth of knowing Christ Jesus my Lord. For his sake I have suffered the loss of all things and count them as rubbish, in order that I may gain Christ and be found in him, not having a righteousness of my own that comes from the law, but that which comes

> through faith in Christ, the righteousness from
> God that depends on faith. (Philippians 3:7–9)

When we look at life from an eternal perspective, the things of the world are less important, our trials and suffering are more bearable, and our hope for an end to suffering and pain is strengthened and reinforced.

This hope of mine is only possible, however, because it is built on the foundation that Jesus Christ is my Lord and Savior. Anyone whose only hope is in the things of this world and the accomplishments amassed during the brevity of a lifetime will be shocked by an eternity of pain and suffering that will cause the good things in life to fade quickly, becoming a distant dream and memory.

Through Scripture, God gave me an eternal perspective of the temporary and fleeting nature of our earthly life pursuits. If we live now with our eternal destination in mind, we can endure anything that God allows into our lives.

Mercy But at Great Cost

LITTLE DID I know at that time that the trials I would face living with my disability were only beginning. But when our lives here on earth come to an end and we move on, the sufferings we thought were so enormous while going through them and our glories we now elate in will seem like nothing compared with the eternal future that awaits us.

The Bible teaches that when our time on earth comes to an end, we will either enjoy eternal glory in heaven or eternal suffering in hell. Our eternal destiny is dependent on our response to God's gift of salvation through the death and resurrection of Jesus.

When we are going through trials, God's mercy is usually the last thing on our minds. But without God's mercy, all hope in the midst of suffering would be pointless.

> Blessed be the God and Father of our Lord Jesus Christ! According to his great mercy, he has caused us to be born again to a living hope through the resurrection of Jesus Christ from the dead, to an inheritance that is imperishable, undefiled, and unfading, kept in Heaven for you, who by God's power are being guarded through faith for a salvation ready to be revealed in the last time. (1 Peter 1:3–5)

Especially when we are going through trials, it is easy to gloss over a passage such as this and move on. In this passage, Peter is marveling at the glory of God and the mercy that God has extended to us through the suffering that Jesus endured during His life and on the cross. So often we take that mercy for granted and focus on the prize of eternal life and salvation. So often, I think, we go about our lives, living for the moment, without truly grasping how great the cost that was paid for that mercy to be available to us.

Jesus willingly chose to humble Himself for us.

> but made himself nothing, taking the form of a servant, being born in the likeness of men. And being found in human form, he humbled himself by becoming obedient to the point of death, even death on a cross. (Philippians 2:7–8)

No man, not the nails, nor anything else in the entire created world had the power to make Him endure the trials He went through and keep Him on the cross, much less put Him there. His love for us was the only thing that drove Him to endure such excruciating pain and torment that no man can even comprehend. Once on the cross, all the wrath of God for the sins of every human being ever created for all of human history—past, present, future—was unleashed on Jesus.

It is no wonder that He cried out, "My God, my God, why have you forsaken me!" Yet, because of that sacrifice, God's mercy and forgiveness can now be extended to us, who have given God such great pain by our rejection of His authority in our lives.

Because Jesus felt the pain of God forsaking Him on the cross, we can embrace the promise that God gave to Moses, to Joshua, and to those who are just and righteous.

> For the Lord loves justice; he will not forsake his saints. They are preserved forever, but the children of the wicked shall be cut off. (Psalms 37:28)

God only sees us as just and righteous if He sees us clothed in Christ's righteousness. That only happens if we have humbled ourselves before God and believe that we are sinful and have no hope of saving ourselves; that Jesus died on the cross to pay the full penalty for our sin. By believing, repenting of the sin that enslaves us, and calling the Lord Jesus our new master, Lord, and Savior, we obtain salvation by the power of His resurrection. If Jesus is our Lord and Savior, by faith in His name, God extends His grace to us, and He no longer sees us in our sin but through the filter of Christ's righteousness.

> Therefore, if anyone is in Christ, he is a new creation; the old has gone, the new has come! (2 Corinthians 5:17)

When our lives in this world come to an end, we will all be judged for how we used the time that God has given us. Anyone who does not humbly accept the gift of salvation offered by God through the sacrifice of Jesus is still in his or her sin and subject to the wrath of God on sin. He or she will be forced to endure eternal separation from God for an eternity of pain, suffering, and torment in hell, where there will be "weeping and gnashing of teeth." Every individual must decide for his or herself. Our lives in this world are short and insignificant compared with an eternity of either God's glory and sharing in Christ's inheritance or hell's torment and suffering.

Yet despite my understanding about eternity and my knowledge that God was with me and loved me, I still had a long road of recovery and therapy ahead of me. My faith would not remove the trials and suffering but would help me to endure. My parents told me that when I heard that I would never regain the use of my legs, I said that I would have to serve the Lord without them. While still in the hospital, I made up my mind to not focus on what I couldn't do but on what I could do, and let God be my guide. As is the case for everything on this earth, my inability to move is temporary, and I can look forward to a new, fully functional body for eternity in heaven. For now, though, I would endure.

My parents researched and visited a few rehab centers located in our general vicinity. I don't remember how much input, if any, I had into this decision, but we eventually decided on a rehab center in Elizabethtown, Pennsylvania, about an hour from our home. After three and a half weeks at Lancaster General Hospital, I left for rehab.

Rehabilitation

THE REHABILITATION CENTER that my parents chose for me was an older facility, then owned by the Penn State Hershey Medical Center. A new facility was under construction on campus in Hershey, Pennsylvania, but for me at least, the center in Elizabethtown would be home for the next three and a half months. It was back in the woods and, being old, had a rustic feel and a pleasant outdoor environment. Inside, it was aged and in need of work, but despite the appearance, it was well suited for the job that it housed. It almost seemed a little, but not much, less "hospital-like" than being within a hospital complex such as Hershey Medical Center or what I experienced the previous three weeks at Lancaster General, and I welcomed it. It was also closer to home than the other locations that were considered, giving my parents and other visitors more frequent access than would have been possible at other facilities.

I was initially in a room with two other patients, one of which was getting ready to go home. Another patient would promptly fill that bed, and that was the way things went during my stay. Patients came and went for varying lengths of time depending on the severity of injury and dedication and determination to learn and improve. As was the case for me most of my life, I interacted well and got along well with everyone, but I did not develop any lasting friendships. At the point of this writing, I have neither contact with nor knowledge of the lives and whereabouts of any patients I rehabbed with at that time. As far as my rehabilitation was concerned, I was determined to make my stay as short as possible and applied the effort I had previously put into gymnastics training over the previous six years to my therapy and rehab. We soon personalized my corner of the room with the cards and pictures that had previously adorned my hospital room at LGH and with posters that my parents brought from home. My parents purchased a TV and VCR for my use at rehab, and they brought in my boom box from home.

My parents helped me get settled into my room and then headed home, an experience different than I had over the previous three weeks. At LGH, I was accustomed to seeing my parents on a daily, almost constant basis. But now I was farther away, and their lives could not be put on hold indefinitely. My parents had my brother to care for, my father had his law practice, and our house would need a lot of work. I was in rehab, not to recover and return to my life as I knew it, but to learn how to adapt and live with my new limitations and to strengthen what muscles I could still control.

I saw my parents a few times a week for the next few months and welcomed home-cooked meals my mother occasionally brought for me. There was one day a week, family day, that family members could watch training movies and attend therapy sessions. Throughout the time I was in the hospital and rehab, my father had cut his time at the law practice by 50 percent. Part of that time he spent visiting rehabs and planning the renovations to the house, but he also visited me at rehab on family day (I think it was Wednesday), one other day in the week, and at least one day every weekend. My mother visited more frequently, but not to the same extent as when I was in Lancaster.

I had other occasional visitors, although I don't recall how frequent. When I did have visitors, I enjoyed spending time outdoors, including walks around the campus. The weather got colder as weeks and months passed, and we spent much less time outside. I have memories of visitors at both LGH and rehab, but at this point, I don't remember who visited at each location. I know I had visits from my gymnastics coaches and some friends from school and church who came to both.

Three distinct visits, however, left a lasting impression on me. The first was from a gymnastics coach from a nearby gymnastics team. But what made this visit special was the guest he brought with him. Vladimir Artemov, the all-around gold medalist in the 1988 Seoul Olympics, was visiting our country from Russia, and he came to see me at rehab! It was an experience I will never forget.

The second was memorable more because of the event itself than who specifically was present. It was an evening in which we had a dance. I used to love to dance and, even though I could no longer move my legs, I was looking forward to it. I also don't recall if the visitors were a surprise or if I was expecting them, but a group of friends came and spent time with me, laughing, reminiscing, and trying to dance with a quadriplegic in a wheelchair.

We had a lot of fun that night. But the event that was most important to me was a visit from my gymnastics coach, Larry. During this visit, I learned from him that following my injury, he came to faith in Christ. He explained that he and a friend were involved in a Bible study. But until the night of my injury, he was not ready to turn his life over to Jesus. With my injury fresh in his mind, he realized that he needed Jesus in his life.

A typical week at the rehab center included physical and occupational therapy almost every day. In physical therapy, I worked on strength, coordination, and flexibility. I worked on things like trying to roll, sit up, and move around on a mat table by using only my arms. I eventually began working on trying to transfer myself into and out of my wheelchair, a task I never accomplished independently. I lifted weights and used machines for strength training. In occupational therapy (OT), I focused on learning adaptations for doing things with limited ability, such as eating, writing, cooking, etc. These tasks required special splints and cuffs to hold utensils. Maneuvering my wheelchair required the rims to be wound with rubber tubing to provide a type of grip to help me push. We worked on getting around a kitchen and using special knives and cooking utensils. Much of what we worked on I have never incorporated into my life, but it was a matter of finding out just how independent I could eventually become.

At first, my wrist flexors were practically nonexistent. In OT, we monitored for signals as I would try to lift my hands by using my wrists. Eventually, the therapist detected trace signals in my right wrist, and we began working to strengthen it. And while I can now move my right wrist, it remains weak, and to this day I have no functional movement of my left wrist. Nevertheless, I have found ways of using both hands and can pick up some small items as needed, even without the ability to move my fingers.

We went on some "field trips" to area stores, restaurants, and movies to experience life in public with our new limitations, but I don't remember specific details about these trips. A couple of times we went swimming. I have very mixed feelings about this unique experience. Once in the water, I enjoyed trying to move around by stretching my hands out as far as I could in front of me and pulling back against the water around me. Forward progress was slow, as I was unable to cup my hands to move the water effectively, but I enjoyed being under the water for as long as I could hold my breath. The caregivers with me would watch for a stream of bubbles that I would blow out to alert that I needed to come up for air. Getting from my wheelchair into the water and getting out, changed, and back into my wheelchair, however, was a hassle and discomfort. After being discharged from rehab, I did go swimming several more times, but soon decided it was more trouble than it was worth.

We had some free time each day, and most weekends I had off, but at least for the first month or two, I was unable to leave the rehab center. On Sunday mornings, I listened to our church service radio broadcast in one of the lounges on my hall. Sometimes my parents visited on Sundays and joined me, but most weeks I listened alone.

With school now in session back home, some of my teachers sent work for me to do at my leisure. In most of my subjects, I was able to keep up with some of my work. German, on the other hand, was difficult. Without the benefit of in-class discussion, I fell woefully behind. Other than schoolwork, I had a TV and books to occupy my free time. I also spent time with other patients. There were games available, and sometimes we just talked. One of my favorite nurses was good at doing the Crytoquip puzzles out of the newspaper, and I came to enjoy working on them during my free time.

When I was injured, I lost all control of my bodily functions, a condition that would, unfortunately, be permanent. Part of spinal cord injury rehabilitation involves bowel and bladder management training. I quickly realized that personal privacy and space were a thing of the past, and I would always be dependent on other people for my care. I would require daily catheterization and scheduled routine bowel programs for the rest of my life.

My first trip away from the rehab center without hospital staff was a trip to Leola, Pennsylvania, not far from my home. Joni Eareckson Tada and Mike King were speaking at the Worship Center, and my parents wanted to take me to hear them.

For me to go, my parents learned my care and how to transfer me into and out of a car. These transfers were required for me to go anywhere. They were difficult, but we had no other options at that time. That day, I met Joni, whose ministry would eventually figure prominently in our family.

During a break at the seminar, an older woman opened the men's restroom door, yelled, "He's coming in!," wheeled in her husband (right behind all the men standing at the urinals), and proceeded to stoop down on the floor in the middle of the restroom and catheterize her husband. Our first exposure to life outside rehab in the world of disability was eye-opening!

After a couple of months of rehab, I was able to go home for a weekend visit. For this visit, my parents had rented a hospital bed that was set up in the living room. I would never see my old second-floor bedroom again,

Our house was undergoing major renovations at this time to accommodate my needs. My parents had a ramp constructed in our garage for wheelchair access to the house. The master bedroom on the main level became my room, and my parents moved to the basement, which had formerly been our family room. They had the doorway to the bedroom widened and installed a two-way swinging door. Renovations to the master bathroom included the addition of a roll-in shower, elongated toilet, and a sink that allowed wheelchair access. We would need to have the work completed before I could come home permanently, but for this first visit, we would suffice with temporary accommodations. Although not required for my return home, my father's former study would soon contain a mat table similar to those I used for therapy at the rehab center.

Aside from the accommodations, there was nothing very memorable that I now recall from that first trip home. It was very quiet overnight and different from what I had become accustomed to in the rehab center. I still required periodic turning from side to side while in bed to avoid developing pressure sores, but I quickly learned that there weren't nurses just walking around checking on patient needs. I was able to get my parents' attention overnight but felt bad that I had wakened them. I learned to measure the importance of my needs and ascertain if what I wanted could wait until morning.

That weekend ended, and I returned to the rehab center. I continued therapy and rehabilitation for the remainder of three and a half months. A couple of weeks before Christmas, I was cleared to go home for good. Admittedly a bit nervous, I was anxious to venture out and experience the new life I would now have. I knew that God was with me and would help me through any challenges I would face.

Back Home and Back to School

Early in December, I learned that I might be able to go home before Christmas. I naturally wanted to spend Christmas at home with my family. The renovations at home would be complete, my rehab was going well, and I was ready to leave.

The decision finally came that I would indeed be going home, but my life at home would be completely different than it had been. Before I could leave, I would need to have attendant care set up at home. I would not have constant nursing care available as at the rehab center, but my needs were significant enough that it was too much for my parents to accept sole responsibility.

I would receive nursing care mornings and evenings, paid for by my father's insurance. This care, initially provided by Kimberly Quality Care, would be enough to help me with getting dressed, transferring me into my wheelchair, and getting me ready to go for the day. Nurses would also help me get to bed each night and with my hygiene and bowel and bladder management.

I had to have a schedule for everything, and spontaneity was no longer possible. Everywhere we went from that point on, I had to factor in my need to cath first thing in the morning, around lunchtime, suppertime, and right before bed, every day without exception. Whenever we would make any plans for an evening activity, we always had to keep in mind that three days a week, I needed to be home for a bowel program that began around 9:00. Other nights I had a little more time, but still had a scheduled attendant arriving for assistance with showering and transferring into bed. My days always began with about an hour and a half of attendant care and ended with either one or two hours of care, depending on the night.

For me to go back to school, I would need to cath at school sometime during each day. In preparation for my return to school, the nurses from Garden Spot High School visited the rehab center for instruction. I would then need to visit the nurse every day at lunchtime.

After being discharged from rehab, I left for home with three wheelchairs and an assortment of supplies, including egg crate mattresses to help prevent pressure sores overnight, splints for my arms and legs, and cuffs for varying purposes. I had a cuff for writing, a cuff for eating, and sandwich holders that I could use for sandwiches or pizza. I had specially adjusted silverware, bent at just the right angle to enable me to get food from a plate to my mouth. I felt, at first, as if I needed to carry a suitcase around with me everywhere I went to accommodate any potential need, which was not a realistic long-term expectation. It didn't take me long to figure out exactly what I would need and what I could do without in the real world. I was soon able to eliminate my need for all but one type of cuff. I found ways to do what I needed with one universal tool, and I eventually learned that I could manage well enough with unadjusted silverware. I still required supplies to cath while away from home, but things were at least somewhat simplified.

We soon replaced the egg crate mattresses that were sent home with me with an alternating chamber air mattress. Due to liability concerns, the rehab center did not permit the use of these items. Instead, they employed staff to roll patients every two hours throughout the night. But in the home, it was our discretion. Using the air mattress enabled me to eventually sleep through the night, undisturbed and without needing to be turned. The mattress alternated between two sets of chambers, filling up with air and releasing in a cyclical pattern and helping to prevent sores from continuous pressure on any given area of my body.

Occasionally, an attendant would forget to turn the pump on or the mattress sprang a leak, but overall I have fared well in avoiding sores. Developing pressure sores meant added time in bed, lying off of the affected area. I have had times in my life since the accident when I have spent the majority of days at a time in bed to allow sores to heal, but those instances have been rare. I think that I've been blessed to have not had more trouble than I have had. Pressure sores are an ongoing concern that can completely consume the lives of individuals with spinal cord injuries.

The wheelchairs I came home with included a shower chair, a manual chair, and a power chair. My newly renovated bathroom at home had a roll-in shower that was able to accommodate the shower chair, and an elongated toilet suitably fitting under the chair. The manual chair was my choice for getting around. Pushing the chair was difficult, especially on the carpet in our home, but in my mind, I think I felt less disabled if I could physically aid in my mobility. For the remainder of my junior and senior years of high school, the power chair did little more than collect dust. My power chair would enable me to go more places more easily, but it felt restrictive. In the manual chair, I felt active, could reach the floor to try to pick things up, and just felt more comfortable. Eventually, I would view the move to the power chair as a gain of independence, but at first, I did not see it that way.

Initially, everywhere I went, I needed to transfer into and out of a car with my wheelchair stashed in either the back seat or the trunk. Eventually, we were gifted by our church with a new Ford Econoline van. Initially purchased as a shell without interior, we had it immediately converted with a lowered floor and chairlift.

In church, the youth group met on the third floor. Each week, I would find my way to the bottom of the stairs and ask for help getting up. Two people, one on either side of me, would carry me in my wheelchair up two flights of stairs and then back down again when finished. Before long, a ramp was constructed to the basement level for our class to move, but for the first couple of months, I relied on others to carry me up and down steps.

A lift-equipped handicapped school bus picked me up outside my house to take me to and from school each day. I was one of two passengers, the one other boy being dropped off at a different school. Once at school, our homeroom assignments were designated according to grade and name in alphabetical order. My room assignment that year was on the second floor. While the school had just recently installed a chairlift, I opted to report to KGSH (the in-school radio station) rather than to navigate the stairs first thing each morning. I would use the lift to get to some of my classes, though, and was proud to have the distinction of being the first to use it.

Our school radio show, under the faculty oversight of Stan Deen, opened up each day with announcements, entertainment, and news that was relevant to our school and community. For the first couple of weeks, I just watched and listened. Eventually, I approached Mr. Deen with the proposition that someone should provide a thought for the day. He approved of the idea and assigned me the task of finding and presenting each day's thought. From then until the end of the year, I quietly became known as the Thought Master.

I presented each day's thought anonymously and, outside of our closed radio crew, did not tell anyone I was doing it. Eventually, classmates recognized me, but the mystery was fun. I bought a book entitled *Peter's Quotations*. Many of my thoughts came from this book, especially at first. Some were my ideas, and some came from the news, articles, movies, and the Bible.

During my senior year, KGSH transitioned to television. I continued to play the role of the Thought Master, but with the added potential TV provided, that role was featured only a couple of times a week rather than daily, and less frequently over time. I contributed, as did all of the crew, with looking for relevant news and public interest stories as well. I researched and presented a few features myself over the course of the year and accepted the role of co-station manager. When I could arrange it, I arrived at school early or stayed late afterward to get things done at the station. I was dependent on my parents driving me either to or from school for this to happen, so it wasn't an everyday occurrence. Most days I rode the bus.

Mr. Deen impacted my life and the lives of many other students during his tenure at Garden Spot. He was an English teacher and oversaw not only KGSH but also GSPA (Garden Spot Performing Arts). I had not known him well until after my injury and never officially took a class with him, but being under his supervision for

KGSH was an encouragement to me as I was trying to find my place and learn to live with a disability in the noninstitutionalized world. Before I was injured, gymnastics took up a lot of my time and was a very significant part of my life. KGSH and the encouragement I received from Mr. Deen helped to fill the void in my life that gymnastics had once occupied. I still went to the gym regularly to help with coaching, but it was by no means as much of a commitment physically, mentally, or emotionally as it had been to compete.

Mr. Deen was a man with a strong faith in Jesus Christ, and I believe it was no coincidence that he played a significant role in my life at this time in my development. His involvement in my life is another indication that God is in control and was helping me to overcome the challenges that my disability provided for me. I would frequently visit Mr. Deen's classroom, and periodically, during free periods, I would audit his classes. His perspective on life, his teaching, and his sense of humor were refreshing changes from the academic track that I chose. I enjoyed sitting back and listening, knowing that I had no responsibilities in the class and nothing to be graded. When choosing my courses, I always scheduled as many advanced placement classes as possible. Mr. Deen's teaching wasn't easy, but it was not as mentally taxing as the AP classes I enrolled in for credit.

I continued my pursuit of art and, despite my physical limitations, enjoyed drawing and other limited artistic avenues of creativity. I couldn't do everything my classmates were doing but did what I could. To this day, we have one of my paintings on the wall of our bedroom. Every once in a great while, I still feel the urge to draw and get out some paper and a pen or pencil.

As mentioned previously, some of my teachers had sent work to the rehab center. As a result, within a short time after returning to school, I was pretty much caught up. Although my mind was still sharp, however, the physical aspect of school work was more difficult and time-consuming than it was before my accident. Tests, in particular, proved difficult because I could not work as fast as I once did. For the most part, my teachers were kind enough to allow me extra time to account for my physical limitations. The one subject that I struggled with most was German, but this had nothing to do with my physical limitations. Having missed in-class discussion time the first third of the year, I struggled with remembering vocabulary and speaking understandably. I always pushed myself very hard, and the thought of repeating German 3 during my senior year was not something that appealed to me. So after returning from the rehab center, I struggled through German 3 and was unable to obtain a good understanding of the material. Then the following year, I had even more trouble in German 4. My pride prevented me from repeating German 3, and I struggled just to get a passing grade. The most futile academic pursuit of my education, I now remember hardly any German at all.

Overall, though, I had always been internally driven to desire success in all my classes, and because things took longer than they used to, I spent a lot of time at home doing homework. When I wasn't in school, doing homework, or otherwise occupied with something related to school or KGSH, I enjoyed reading and watching movies, two things I still enjoy. I especially liked reading about and studying anything related to Christian apologetics.

My faith was a significant part of my life, and I was increasingly finding that there was more to the Bible than mere blind faith. The authenticity and cohesiveness of the Bible are outstanding. There is no comparison in all of literature. There is more proof for the authenticity and truth of the Bible than for all other pieces of ancient literature combined, and I am unaware of any contradictions or challenges that do not have a reasonable explanation. I spent hours reading to learn as much as possible about Christianity and the Bible. I have found that the Bible is accurate and in agreement with observable and historical science and in all matters of historical and archeological data. Apologetics has been a hobby of mine ever since, and the Bible is not merely a hobby, but a part of my daily life.

Despite being a quadriplegic, I have not always been as cautious as I should have been. I was known for trying to do more than I was physically capable of and, on occasion, got myself into trouble. More than once, my parents came home to find me on the floor, having tried to pick something up or from just plain carelessness on my part. One thing I enjoyed was trying to pop wheelies in my chair. And although there were anti-tip wheels on the back, occasionally they were forgotten, and I would flip over backward. We also had a ramp in our garage leading up into the house. This ramp was a challenge to me that I continually worked to master. On one occasion, however, I gave a big push and leaned back too far, the chair flipping back and over the anti-tip wheels. My head hit the concrete garage floor, and I was left lying flat on my back calling for help until somebody found me. I was fortunate to have never been seriously hurt, but looking back, I wonder if I have memory problems that stemmed from hitting my head too often. Despite the dangers and accidents, I had enough success in my endeavors for independence that I continued to test my limitations. I had to learn just how far I could push myself.

Garden Spot was designed in the shape of a U, with the high school on one side and the junior high on the other, connected in the middle by the auditorium. Ramps at either side of the auditorium lobby provided access from the high school, situated at the highest elevation, to the junior high at the lowest. Pushing myself up the ramps was difficult and a test of my strength and determination, but going down was fun. At first, I wasn't able to control the speed of my chair going down forward. Initially, I backed the chair down the ramp, but I soon began testing myself to determine how much I could handle rolling forward. I frequently had to make a left-hand turn at the bottom and learned that if I timed it right, I could lean to the left just before the hallway, clamp the left wheel with my arm, and slide around the corner. Then, if I released my grip at the right time, I could roll down the hall without hitting the wall. Most of the time, I navigated successfully. On one occasion, however, I was off track and hit the wall. I wasn't going extremely fast, but enough that when my feet hit, my chair tipped forward and my forehead kissed the wall. The only thing hurt was my pride, even though I don't think anyone saw the incident.

At home, we resided near the top of a slow-graded rise. Once, on a walk with a friend, I let my chair go. She began walking beside me, then jogging, running, and finally watching me continue picking up speed as I careened down the hill ahead of her. At the bottom, the slope leveled off, and my friend caught up, but it was probably faster than I had gone in a wheelchair at any other time in my life. Looking back on the incident, I recognize how dangerous it was, but at the time it was fun. I know now that one small stone under my front wheel could have easily flipped me out of my chair. Years later, I visited Garden Spot HS, and after looking at the ramp from a more mature perspective, I think I was crazy doing what I did. With maturity, I gained a little more sense and reservation, but like any teenager, even despite my accident and disability, I did not recognize all the dangers inherent in my decisions at the time.

All in all, living in the real world with a disability was humbling, especially for a teenager. I had to learn to rely on others a lot during a time in life in which most of my peers were beginning to assert their independence. I learned that I did indeed have some good friends who were willing to do for me whatever I needed. God blessed me with friends who were always looking out for my needs. I even had a couple of friends who were willing to assist with my catheterization, enabling me to go on school field trips and even an overnight retreat with the youth group.

It was difficult getting around. Physically doing my school and homework was hard. Although I shared, to a degree, in the successes of others, it was hard seeing other people engaging in activities I once enjoyed. Although infrequent, it was embarrassing dealing with bowel or bladder accidents over which I had no control. While I tried to hide these occurrences and feelings, I know that they did not go entirely unnoticed. I do not, however, recall anyone critically looking down on me in the aftermath of these instances, and I did not let my trials define who I was.

By that point in my life, God had convinced me that He was in control of all things. He had also blessed me with the ability to see my life from the perspective of eternity, that everything we experience now is insignificant compared with the eternal glory awaiting Jesus' followers in heaven. Focusing on the problems would have undoubtedly left me depressed. But the perspective with which God enabled me to view my life allowed me to focus on Jesus and His goodness in the midst of my struggles.

My high school years came to an end, and it was time for graduation. I graduated sixth in my class. At graduation, I gave a commencement speech in which I gave the final words from the "Thought Master." I was enrolled to begin college at Franklin and Marshall College the following fall and was looking forward to the new challenges that awaited me.

Summer Activity, Joni and Friends, and the Tim Weaver Invitational

THE SUMMER BETWEEN my junior and senior years of high school was in many ways similar to years past, but my disability added a new dimension to everything we did. In prior years, gymnastics occupied much of my time. I had also started my first paid position, working as a dishwasher at a local restaurant. This year, these responsibilities were combined into one as I began working part-time as a coach at Positive Fitness, the gym for which I had competed. It was strange to me to receive a paycheck from the gym, but it did allow me to remain active in the sport I had grown to love. I don't know that I was a particularly good coach, but I did enjoy being there and providing any input that I could.

Working at the gym, however, only accounted for a small part of my week. When I wasn't at the gym, I spent as much time as possible sitting outside, reading and drawing. I preferred the outdoors, especially on sunny days, because I did not like air conditioning. Since my accident, my body has been unable to regulate temperature properly. As a result, I have had difficulty staying warm. Therefore, I spent as much time as possible in the sun and out of air conditioning. I did have to be careful, however, because I also no longer sweat to cool my body and could easily overheat. If we were away from home, knowing we would be out in the heat for long periods of time, we frequently carried spray bottles of water to cool me. While my body has somewhat adjusted to colder temperatures over the years, I still prefer to be warm and frequently wear sweatshirts year-round when the majority of my day is in air conditioning.

As a family, we still went to the beach for vacations, but there was no vacation from my disability. Even away from home, I required daily care. Becky, who had been one of my nurses in the hospital, became a friend of our family. We did a lot together during the first few years after my accident. She joined us on many trips and took much of the burden off my parents.

Rather than spending a lot of time on the beach as I had grown up doing, I spent much of my time on the porch of our beach house, reading and drawing. Just seeing the ocean was enough for me.

Various activities we undertook while away required me to be lifted out of my chair and carried onto boats and, on one occasion, an airplane. At that point in my life, I desired to engage myself in as many activities as possible, but with time, I grew to dislike anything that required me to be out of my wheelchair. Getting out of my chair is uncomfortable, and I honestly don't feel there is much I miss out on by staying in my chair.

That first summer after I was injured, Joni Eareckson Tada's ministry, Joni and Friends, organized a Family Retreat at Spruce Lake Retreat in the Poconos, Pennsylvania. After his recent experience in dealing with my injury, my father, an attorney, presented a seminar on the legal ramifications of living with a disability. He entitled it "Mastering the Maze." This first exposure to Joni and Friends opened the door to many years of interaction and participation in Joni and Friends' ministry. After we had attended Joni and Friends' Family Retreat for a couple of years, my father joined Sib Charles in running the retreat at Spruce Lake. A couple of years later, he left his law practice and accepted the position of Area Director for Joni and Friends Eastern Pennsylvania, a new area office that would take over the administration of the Family Retreat at Spruce Lake and other related ministry needs.

Within a few years of its inception, the Family Retreat expanded from one week to three weeks that were spread out over the summer.

The additional weeks enabled many more families to benefit from the program. There was a Walk'n Roll to raise money for Joni and Friends each year. By this time in my life, I had graduated from college and was working at Lancaster Laboratories. For many years, I went around the building at work and asked for donations for the fundraiser. I expended much effort and took great pride in trying to raise the most for an individual. I think, in a way, I felt a sense of obligation to gather as much support as possible since my father was the Area Director.

While at the Family Retreat that summer, I learned of an "Overcomers Camp" that would convene at Spruce Lake later in the summer. Although outside my comfort zone, I decided to attend. It was a fun week, and the following year I went again, but that was my last. We would go to Family Retreat through 2003, but at the time of this writing, we have not been back since. For several of those years, the last being in 1998, we also traveled to Bonclarken, North Carolina for a second Family Retreat where our family joined a team of volunteers to serve, while simultaneously being served ourselves.

Looking back on our history with Joni and Friends, it's amazing how God took us from being served that first year to being in a position to reciprocate that service to others in the midst of my disability. God used my father's expertise in law as a doorway into ministry, leading our whole family to embrace Joni and Friends as a new part of our lives. Several years later, my wife and I organized the youth program at the retreat for one year. That was difficult for me, and I'm not sure that I would make a good program director. I did and still do enjoy teaching, however, and welcomed the opportunity to test myself.

In 2006, my father stepped down as Area Director, and our involvement with Joni and Friends came to an end. Today, he remains active in disability ministry as a board member of Handi*Vanglism Ministries International.

Joni Eareckson Tada has a powerful testimony, and Joni and Friends is still a thriving ministry to this day. There are now area ministries and Family Retreats all across the nation. Through Joni and Friends' Wheels for the World ministry, thousands of wheelchairs are collected, refurbished, and delivered to those in need around the world. My family is no longer actively involved with Joni and Friends, but that ministry had been a big part of our lives for many years and still ministers to millions of people around the world. We played a bit part in a ministry that spans the globe, but it was a part that we enjoyed while it lasted.

While my father was still involved with Joni and Friends, we nearly lost him when he contracted pancreatitis. God blessed us with thousands of prayers that went up to God on his behalf, as word of my father's condition spread through the network of people associated with Joni and Friends. We found out after the fact that these prayers came from people praying for him as far away as China. The doctors thought his chances of living were small, but he survived and is alive today. God is awesome.

In the fall following my injury, a gymnastics club running out of the Hanover YMCA held the First Annual Tim Weaver Invitational, a gymnastics competition set up in my honor to raise money toward medical expenses and other needs incurred because of my injury. It was a lot of fun, and I enjoyed helping with the announcing throughout the two-day event. For many years, this was an annual reunion with gymnasts, coaches, and judges that I looked forward to and enjoyed. God had given me a platform, and I was able to share my testimony with those in attendance. While my involvement eventually stopped, the meet itself is still an annual event as of the time of this writing. The Tim Weaver Battlefield Invitational has now expanded to a three-day event and features both boys and girls events. In 2018, there were more than 1,400 competitors at the competition held at the York Expo Center in York, Pennsylvania.

At the Pennsylvania State Championship each year, the graduating seniors were recognized before exiting the program and moving on to either college or employment. In my senior year of high school, although I could not compete, I still attended with my team. I was surprised when the announcer called my name to join the other competitors on the floor even though I had not competed in two years. I received the award for the Most Distinguished Senior, a truly humbling experience.

During that first summer, a representative from Kimberly Quality Care, the nursing agency hired for my attendant care, contacted me regarding the opportunity to feature in an ad campaign that would run in the Wall Street Journal and Newsweek magazine. Of course, I said yes. A few weeks later in the gym, a camera crew set up and captured my image with the backdrop of one of my teammates on the high bar.

After graduating from high school, I began attending the college and career Sunday school class at our church. An annual class activity was a weekend retreat at Harvey Cedar's Bible Conference. I don't remember much about the event, but that weekend at the beach was when I first met Geri, the young lady who would eventually become my wife.

Indeed, God is good, and I have been truly blessed. It is only by His grace and His mercy that I am where I am today. Despite my limitations and difficulties, it is comforting to know that God is in control of every aspect of my life. It is comforting to know that when my time here on earth comes to an end, I can look forward to an eternity to bask in the glory of my God, my Lord, and my Savior. To Him, I give all praise and glory for all my worldly accomplishments and for the privilege of allowing Him to live and work in and through me.

Learning to Drive

Toward the end of my senior year of high school, I began the process of learning to drive. I was sixteen at the time of my accident, and I remember lying in the hospital bed realizing that my driver's permit was expiring. Two years later, PennDOT renewed it without requiring me to retake the written test. I was relieved and ready to begin training.

Although provided with a power wheelchair when I left the rehab center, I utilized a manual wheelchair throughout my high school years. Driving, however, would require full-time use of the power chair. The manual chair would not provide the stability I needed within the van. It wasn't a hard decision, as I would also need the power chair at college, but it was a decision that I had to make. I was moving into a new phase of my life, requiring a changing lifestyle.

An evaluation at Hershey Medical Center verified my ability to control a motor vehicle and determined what modifications would be needed. The evaluator's van could be customized to accommodate the varying needs of each applicant. A lift provided access for me and my wheelchair, and I pulled my chair into the driver's seat position. The floor height under the driver's seat was adjustable to position the driver exactly where needed. A single-hand control, a tri-pin joystick box stuck to the door with Velcro for precise positioning, controlled the brake and accelerator.

The steering wheel was on an extended column that could be adjusted side to side and up and down, as well as providing the means to twist and tilt the wheel for positioning at different angles. The steering wheel itself had multiple-size options to accommodate the varying range of motion between applicants. An attachment for a joystick allowed for single-hand steering without ever letting go of the wheel. The pressure that was required to engage the accelerator and brake, as well as the resistance for steering, could be customized to adjust for the strength of each applicant.

The initial evaluation provided the list of modifications that would be needed for me to drive. I would require a small steering wheel positioned at an angle to my right and with zero effort steering. The accelerator and brake would be controlled by my left hand through the use of a joystick permanently attached to the driver's door. Buttons positioned at my left elbow to control the turn signals, wipers, and horn could be hit as needed while driving. These completed modifications should enable me to operate a vehicle safely and successfully. I attended practice sessions until I felt comfortable with driving, and the instructor felt comfortable with approving my training. The practice sessions initially took place on an open lot, but soon included varied traffic conditions and roadways.

With one exception, my training was without incident. On one trip, however, I was driving on relatively narrow streets with cars parked on both sides. I got too close to the cars on the right side, and my passenger side mirror smacked the mirror of a parked pickup truck. The van mirror flew into the van through the open passenger window and landed on the instructor's lap. Fortunately, the pickup truck mirror was not damaged, but the training van needed repairs.

Once the instructor and I were comfortable with my progress, I was ready to take the driver's test. The conversion of my van, to be based on the specifications compiled by the evaluator, would not occur until after I passed the test. Because driving would be an asset to my eventual employment, the driver's evaluation and van conversion were paid for by the Pennsylvania Office of Vocational Rehabilitation (OVR). Understandably, OVR would not pay to have the conversion done until they were sure that I would be able to drive.

On the day of my driver's test, the instructor and I went to the police barracks for the test, and an officer and I went out onto the driving course. He was interested in the vehicle and all that was involved in the conversion and my ability to drive. When it came time to parallel park, I began backing into the space. As I neared the curb, I commented that I wasn't sure that I could back up any farther. I noted that if I hit the curb, I would fail the test. The officer assured me that if I avoided the cones, I would not fail. As it turned out, I did hit the curb, quickly adjusted, and maneuvered into place. None of the cones that were set up marking out the space were touched, however, and I passed the test without any other difficulties. In April 1992, I received my driver's license. OVR received the report and requested bids to initiate the process for converting my van. A company in Harrisburg, Pennsylvania, Haveco, won the job and completed the conversion of my van on November 11, 1992.

When I got my van back, however, I found that I was unable to drive it safely. I don't know what was different between my van and the training van, but a "blind spot" in the steering prevented me from recovering from left-hand turns. I nearly had a couple of scary accidents and I'm thankful that God saved me from crashing.

On one occasion, I pulled out, turning left onto a busy Route 23, the steering locked and I made a U-turn, headed back across the oncoming lane and nearly off the side of the road from which I'd initially come. There was a remote brake installed in the van for training purposes. Had my father not pressed the button when he did, we would have careened off the side of the road, through a fence, and into a field. By God's grace, no oncoming traffic was close and unable to stop before hitting us, there was no damage done, and nobody was injured. Nevertheless, the incident shattered my confidence, and I had developed a real fear of turning left into traffic. That was not the last time that I had trouble recovering from left-hand turns, but that was the worst incident, and from then on I was always prepared to hit the brakes.

On another occasion, I was traveling along a highway that was veering to the left. The degree of the turn was just enough that I had to hold my hand at the two o'clock position on the steering wheel to stay on the road. This position was right at the spot at which I was frequently getting stuck. I was unable to hold to the curve and drifted toward the guardrail. My father reached over, pushed the wheel where it belonged, and kept us pointed in the right direction.

My father and I spent significant time on weekends practicing and experimenting with the steering column and wheel positioning to try to solve the problems with my driving. Sunday afternoons, we spent hours at Greenfield Industrial Park business complex. With most businesses closed, there was very little traffic and ample space to practice. At a point when we were nearly out of ideas and I was wondering if I would ever be able to safely and comfortably drive, I came up with a possible solution. A strap anchored on the left-hand push handle on my wheelchair, going around my right shoulder, and connecting to my left armrest behind the joystick would keep my weight from shifting to the right during left-hand turns and keep my arm in a position where I could utilize my full range of motion to steer. My father and the technicians at the garage were skeptical of my solution, but we nevertheless pursued the matter with the occupational therapy group at Hershey Medical Center.

After receiving the completed strap, we returned to Greenfield Industrial Park for testing. I made turn after turn to test my ability to recover from left-hand turns. On one occasion, I turned so fast and sharp that my dad and Geri thought I was trying to roll the van. They were thrown up against the passenger side windows until I recovered and straightened out. They never let me live that one down.

The strap did, indeed, keep my body positioned that I was able to drive, but it was not easy for me to put on independently. At first, I struggled for significant periods of time trying to get it on, but I knew that it was necessary if I was to be independent in my ability to get out on my own. Even with this strap, however, it took a long time for my confidence to develop to a point where I felt comfortable going anywhere by myself. Eventually, I did become confident enough to venture out on my own. For the entire time that I had the van, however, I avoided driving on narrow streets and stayed out of the city as much as possible. Over time, the Velcro strap gradually weakened and became increasingly less effective, but the change was gradual enough that I was slowly able to wean myself away from the necessity of using it. The more time I spent driving, the more I was able to anticipate when I would have difficulty and could compensate to avoid serious problems. But as long as I had the van, I never fully felt comfortable without the strap.

College

DURING MY SENIOR year of high school, I began to think seriously about my life after graduation. Before my accident, I had always assumed that I would go to college. I hadn't given any thought to a course of study, but I knew that I wanted to compete in gymnastics somewhere. Now that gymnastics was no longer an option, the only questions were where I would go and what I would study. I enjoyed art and mathematics and, for a while, considered a career in architecture. My father thought that I should do something with computers as that field would offer the best adaptations for my disability, but I didn't give it serious consideration. I didn't have a good reason for not considering it. It just didn't appeal to me at the time.

I requested information on several colleges and universities within the Lancaster, Pennsylvania, area. In large part because of my disability and my dependence on others, the thought of leaving the comforts of home and the attendant care resources and schedule I had set up at home was intimidating. Despite my trepidation, I knew that I wanted more than mere existence, living under my parents' roof for the rest of my life. I knew that I needed to find some means of supporting myself to be able to move out on my own. I had met other quadriplegics who lived "independently," and I knew that I could as well.

After reviewing the available resources, I visited and applied to Messiah College and Franklin & Marshall College. When visiting, I was interested primarily in how I would manage my care at each facility. While I recognized that the college would not be responsible for my attendant care, the facility needed to be accommodating and flexible to provide an environment suitable for incoming care.

After serious contemplation, I decided that F&M addressed my needs most effectively. The administration at F&M seemed very willing to go out of their way to make my dorm room accommodating. F&M sent its director of buildings and grounds to visit my home to see the adaptations we made there to meet my needs. Much of the information he gleaned from that visit was used to adapt my room at F&M. A reserved parking space close to my dormitory door assured that my van would be nearby. I had two rooms on either side of a private bathroom. An attendant could stay overnight if needed. Not only was F&M close to home, meaning I would be able to continue using some familiar attendants to begin the year, but I could also recruit new attendants over the summer before starting school. Recruiting attendants would have been difficult to do in advance at Messiah. I would also be able to continue attending my home church throughout my college education, and my parents were accessible in an emergency. Altogether, choosing F&M provided me the opportunity to venture out of the comforts of my home, while at the same time allowing me to hold onto a level of support I would not have had at Messiah.

Even though I was leaving home, my daily routine still required that I have personal care attendants in the mornings and evenings as well as help at lunchtime and dinner time. I had no hesitation asking for help from fellow students with meals in the dining hall, but I still needed to be catheterized four times per day, and that was a bit too personal to ask just anybody. In a dorm room of my own, I also required help with cleaning and laundry each week. I found some people through our church and took advantage of campus-wide email to recruit new workers.

While I was at college, OVR paid for my attendant care. Over the summer and other breaks, a combination of my father's insurance company and United Cerebral Palsy of Lancaster County (UCP) handled it. OVR also provided two computers for my use at college: a desktop computer that I would use in my room and a laptop to take to class. They were both Apple Macintosh computers, as that was the platform adopted by the college over Windows-based systems. I had a Velcro strap that I connected over my lap between the two arms of my wheelchair, enabling me to attach the laptop onto my lap to take notes in class without worrying that the computer would fall. I could type one key at a time using the eraser end of pencils strapped onto each of my hands. For some of my classes, I used the computer to take notes, and for some, I tried to take handwritten notes. In many of my classes, especially math, I borrowed and copied notes from friends to supplement what I was able to gather myself. Taking notes on a computer was most difficult in my math classes.

While many students become heavily involved in school activities and the college life, I was there primarily to get an education, and I studied hard to do well. In the spring and fall, I frequently took my laptop or books outside to work in the sun in locations shielded from the wind. If you recall, it has been an ongoing struggle since my accident to keep warm due to poor circulation and inability of my body to properly regulate temperature. During the winter, I did a lot of studying sitting beside a space heater that the college provided for my room. If I was in the room, it was almost always running. At times my room was probably one of the warmest places on campus.

Each morning, I would have anything that I thought that I might need for the day set out on my bed, desk, or bedside table. In this way, I had access to just about anything that I needed without requiring constant help each day. I wasn't shy about asking for assistance from others on the dorm floor, but I tried to be as independent as possible.

Each night, I had my laptop and books positioned on my bedside table where I could reach from bed after my attendant left. I would often bring back coffee from the dining hall, which I would heat up right before bed to carry me into the night. Frequently, I would sit up in bed studying or working on assignments into the early morning hours. I had a very irregular sleep schedule during my years at F&M, working into the night and occasionally taking a nap during the day as needed. Since I was unable to get myself into and out of bed, I slept during the day by raising my bed and leaning over against the raised bed with a cover pulled over my head.

Because of my disability, examinations in the classroom were difficult. On many occasions my professors allowed me to do my work in my dorm room, where I was not as restricted in my ability to work. I tried not to take advantage of the generosity of my professors and to live up to the trust they put in me. There were times, however, that I felt that I received an unfair advantage and had more time than I should've had to complete my work in comparison to the time given to those in the classroom. My professors rarely gave me time limits, as neither they nor I knew how to compare my limitations in my ability to work with what I would be able to do if I could physically keep up. Working outside the classroom also presented temptations that others in the classroom would not have had. We are all born sinners, and learning to deal with temptation is part of life. As I continued growing and developing as an individual and in my faith, God used this time in my life to help me understand the high priority that integrity needs to hold in one's life, and I am proud of what I accomplished in school.

I don't recall a whole lot about my course schedule during my tenure at F&M. As was the case with most students, I took four classes per semester. Before arriving my freshman year, the one course that I was most excited about taking was Introduction to Philosophy. I was looking forward to studying under the direction of Prof. Michael Murray, a Christian man who had gotten his foot in the door of the Philosophy Department at F&M and was trying to earn tenure. He had visited our church that previous spring and his life inspired me. I was excited about taking my hobby in apologetics to the college level and testing and building my faith. I was confident that my foundational beliefs were correct, and I had complete confidence in the historical and theological reliability of God's Word. I was most excited to find out how God would bolster my faith through what I would learn.

Of my three other classes that year, the only one that I remember is an art class that I almost took. My schedule included the course for only a brief time. Shortly after arriving on campus, I learned that we would be drawing live nude models. I knew that I would not be comfortable with the work and promptly changed my schedule. I also decided that a class in drawing would be difficult, time-consuming, and inconsequential to anything that I would eventually do for a living.

When the time came to declare a major, I seriously considered majoring in philosophy. That was what my heart desired and where I thought I would find the most enjoyment, but I decided that in the end, mathematics would provide more opportunities for eventual employment. I did pick up philosophy as a minor and ended up taking four out of the six required classes under the teaching of Dr. Murray. I often joke that I minored in Murray.

On campus, students had the opportunity to join various clubs and activities outside of their regular curriculum. Throughout the four years that I attended F&M, I was a part of the Inter-Varsity Christian Fellowship and the philosophy club. Being so near home and the church in which I grew up, I was more involved with the college and career Sunday school class and related activities at church than those on campus.

During my time at F&M, I made a few friends who shared an interest in *Star Trek*. *Star Trek: The Next Generation* was in the second to last year of its first-run syndication during my freshman year at college. *Deep Space 9* would begin my sophomore year and *Voyager* my senior year. I did not have a TV in my room. Instead, each week I joined friends in the suite of an upperclassman we all knew as Captain Marc. He and his suitemates became good friends. Most of them graduated a year earlier than I did, however, and were not around through all four years of my college life.

Another friend that I made my freshman year was Rick, the resident assistant (RA) on my floor. I enjoyed visiting his room as he had, if I recall correctly, *seven* fish tanks of various sizes. The largest was a fifty-gallon tank housing an African puffer. He had two twenty-gallon aquariums with fancy goldfish he had named Jesus and Muhammad, and another with a beta named Buddha. He eventually fed most of his fish, including those three, to the puffer fish. He also used to feed the puffer hotdogs, that is, until it decided to go after his finger instead! He was a senior that year and graduated, but we remained in contact another year or two longer as he moved into a nearby apartment complex in Lancaster after graduation. The following year, I felt sorry for his room's new occupants. The dorm continued to smell a little fishy well into the year.

While in college, I also began developing an interest in sports, specifically professional football and basketball, and Notre Dame College football. I don't at this point remember how I got interested in basketball, but because I didn't have a TV in my room, I was limited to following sports online. The Internet at that time was very new. It was also revolutionary that I would have access to a new campus-wide computer network and direct connection to the Internet.

Without having any prior association with any professional sports teams, I decided to follow the San Antonio Spurs because of the reputation and testimony of David Robinson. Some games I could listen to through an online audio feed, but most of the time I was limited to the information I obtained from online live box scores and play-by-play transcription. I even went so far as to increase the font size on my computer monitor and set up macros on the computer to continually refresh and scroll down so that I could follow games that would end after I was in bed. Wi-Fi had not yet been invented, so even though I had my laptop on my bedside table, it did not have Internet access at that time.

My interest in Notre Dame football began because Professor Murray was a Notre Dame alumnus. Not that I ever remember him being in a bad mood, but he seemed to be in better spirits Monday mornings following a Notre Dame win over the weekend. So each Sunday during college football season, I began looking up the box score for Notre Dame's game the previous day. After I graduated, I started watching games and have done so ever since.

Engagement

Recruiting and hiring new attendants has always seemed like a never-ending process. One of my classmates at F&M was a fellow gymnastics teammate from when I competed. Midway through my freshman year following a discussion about my caregiver needs, I hired Mark to work for me. Not long after he started, his roommate, Webb, began as well. When Mark explained what he did, Webb said, "I could do that," and he and Mark became two of my most consistent and reliable attendants during my time at F&M.

It was also during my freshman year that I hired Geri for a couple of mornings a week. I had first met her the previous summer at Harvey Cedars Bible Conference through the college and career Sunday school class. I hadn't gotten to know her very well that weekend, but our family friend, Becky, thought that Geri would work well as an attendant. But not only was she a good caregiver, within a couple of months we began dating, and her role as my attendant quickly changed. Once I was able to find enough other caregivers, she served in a backup role only when needed.

We dated throughout my four years in college, which is part of the reason why I felt I was more involved with the college and career Sunday school class at church than with the college activities at F&M. But she was frequently on campus, and many of my friends there became hers as well. We shared an interest in *Star Trek* and *The X-Files*, and it was now that my interest in professional football began to develop. Geri had grown up following the Dallas Cowboys. As I had no prior allegiance to any particular team, it was easy for me to join her in cheering for the Cowboys. Her father, born in Green Bay and having grown up in Wisconsin, was a Green Bay Packers fan. Since they are in two different divisions and not significant rivals, it was easy to root for both teams. The only conflicts that occurred were when they met in the playoffs and usually one regular season game. In those cases, it was Cowboys all the way! Geri joined our family over the summers when we went on vacation to Joni and Friends Family Retreats. Leading up to Christmas my senior year, I prepared to ask Geri to marry me. I discussed this first with my father since I would need his help in obtaining a ring. I planned to purchase from a jeweler located in Lancaster City. At that point in my life, I was not at all comfortable driving on narrow streets and avoided city driving at all costs. On this occasion, it was unavoidable, so I let my father do the driving. Before making the trip, however, I traveled by myself to Geri's parents' house, invited her father into my van, expressed my intention to marry his daughter, and asked his permission. He granted his approval, and I began making plans.

My father drove my brother and me into the city to purchase an engagement ring. We parked outside the jewelry shop and, because the store was not wheelchair accessible, the store manager brought trays of diamonds, bands, and other gems out and into my van. Knowing that Geri liked emeralds, I found a diamond with a diamond and emerald wrap that I thought she would like. I found an ornament for the Christmas tree that was filigree/blown glass that would camouflage the ring, placed the ring on top around its hangar, and had it hung high on our tree.

The night that I had planned to propose, my parents and brother went to the movies and left the two of us at home. We watched *The Sound of Music* together that night. When it was over, I pulled out a poem that I had written ending with direction to the tree. Geri found the ring on the tree, and I asked her to marry me. I'm embarrassed to say, however, that I did not recite the poem to her out loud. My nerves left me speechless, and I found myself letting her read it for herself before directing her to the tree and asking for her hand in marriage. A funny side story was that my parents and brother were suffering throughout the movie, the theater freezing due to a broken heating system. They stayed, nonetheless, to give the two of us privacy and time.

Despite my trepidation, she said yes. A wedding, however, would not be quickly forthcoming. Before we could get married, I knew that I needed first to graduate, find a job, and find a place in which to live. Only then would we be able to set a date to be married.

Graduation

ONE DAY, ON my way to class, I passed by a dead squirrel on the walkway. When I came back through again later, the squirrel was gone but in its place was a chalk outline of the squirrel. I always got a laugh out of that, and fortunately, my time at F&M ended better than that of that squirrel.

At this point in my life, I don't recall what year or semester this occurred, nor was it vitally significant to my education. Nevertheless, it was a memory that has stuck with me throughout the years, much like the memory of an endeavor I undertook midway through my time at F&M. Several times each year, I get calls from the alumni telephone solicitation committee, of which I was a part for a short amount of time. For one semester, I traveled over a bridge, once present over Harrisburg Pike, one or two evenings a week to make phone calls and try to solicit donations from Franklin & Marshall alumni. Most of the time, those called were very pleasant to talk to, and some shared of their time at F&M. But while it was interesting, and something I'm glad that I took the time to experience, I was not at all disappointed to give it up.

Preceding my senior year of college, my memories of my classes are very limited. One I remember taking, but remember very little about, was a course on the Art of East Asia. It was brutal, scheduled right after lunch, and 90 percent of the class time was in the dark looking at pictures of pottery and sculpture on the screen. I had the hardest time staying awake in that class even though I was always sitting right up in front. I don't recall that I did poorly in the class, but it was a struggle. I also remember taking a government class, but given that I was majoring in math and minoring in philosophy, most of my classes were in those two disciplines.

In the first semester of my senior year, I took the Intro to Computer Science class. Midway through the semester, I wished that I had accepted my father's advice and enrolled in the course earlier in my education. I discovered that I did enjoy working with computers and decided that finding an occupation as a computer programmer would be my postgraduation goal. For the second semester of that year, I took three more programming classes and a final philosophy class to complete my graduation requirements.

Two of my classes that semester were independent studies, one being a mathematical modeling class using Mathematica. The other was a philosophy class in which I presented a paper entitled, "Is This Threat For Real? A Look at the Implications of an Errant Scripture." I thoroughly enjoyed researching and writing this paper, although as I read over it now, I question some of my conclusions. Nevertheless, it was an enjoyable undertaking and it stretched my mind as I wrestled with the issues surrounding an inerrant Scripture.

I also enjoyed my independent study in computer modeling, but the computer class that I had the most fun with was an object-oriented programming class using script X. My final project was a game similar to *Yahtzee*. It was even set up with cheat codes to roll five of a kind and other rolls on demand. The completed program was more than what was required, but I was motivated to do well given my goal of postgraduation employment.

As I was nearing the end of my senior year, I began weighing the options of what to do after graduating. I could go on for further education, or I could look for a job right away. Neither Geri nor I was thrilled with the prospect of graduate school. I did not like the idea of starting over at a new school that would most likely not be in Lancaster County. Starting over, under those circumstances, would mean not having the conveniences I had four years earlier when starting off at F&M. The biggest obstacle would be finding attendant care from scratch. I'm not sure why, but I did not consider Millersville University as an option at that time, but even that was farther than I was sure any of my current attendants would want to travel. Graduate school would also mean putting off a wedding for at least four more years and potentially dealing with a long-distance relationship until completing my degree, neither of which appealed to me.

I decided to look for a job in the area first and see what options would be available locally before looking into any further education. I developed a resume and sent copies of a letter with my resume to as many local businesses as possible. I did receive a few interview opportunities, and by the time I finished my senior year, I had lined up an internship at Lancaster Laboratories at the western edge of Leola, Pennsylvania, not far from where I lived.

On May 19, 1996, I graduated from F&M cum laude. I received the Noss Prize in philosophy for the work I had done on my independent study and was one of seven presented with the John Hershner Scholarship Award for my work in mathematics.

However, I would not have long to relax. Two weeks after graduation, on June 3, 1996, I began my internship at Lancaster Laboratories. I worked as an intern for three months. At the end of that time, I accepted an offer for full-time employment and have been there ever since. I began my work at Lancaster Laboratories with development in DOS using Clarion and Basic. As the lab adopted platform migrated through Windows NT, Windows XP, and then Windows 7 and 10, I learned PowerBuilder, Visual Basic, VB.net, and have begun learning C#.net. Over the years, these have been my primary development tools. On my own at home, I have dabbled in Java and Android development.

Finding a Home

AT CHRISTMAS TIME during my senior year of college, Geri and I were engaged to be married. But before we could set a date for a wedding, three things needed to happen: I had to graduate from college, I had to find a job, and we needed to have a place to live. Adequate planning was needed primarily because of my disability, although in actuality it's not a bad practice to follow for anyone looking for stability in marriage.

Following my graduation and acceptance of full-time employment at Lancaster Laboratories, we began searching for a home that would provide a relatively short commute for me to get to work. Whereas most newly married couples have the luxury of living in an apartment as their first place of residence, my disability required that we employ a bit more upfront planning. In our area at the time, we were aware of only one apartment complex that had one available apartment even remotely suitable for a quadriplegic, and that was in Lancaster City. At the time, driving in the city was something I avoided at all costs.

With the slim likelihood of finding a house adapted suitably for my disability, we felt that we had two options. We could modify an existing home or design and build from scratch. We investigated both possibilities simultaneously, visiting new housing developments as well as homes that were on the market. We seriously considered a plot in a new development just up the street from Lancaster Laboratories, but various zoning delays derailed that option.

Then one day we found a house listed for public sale that was only a five-minute drive from Lancaster Laboratories. It was not easily accessible for me to get into the house, so Geri and my father visited first. They were both very excited about this small ranch house, and we scheduled a second visit for me to see the house. Whereas most ranch houses feature a narrow hallway that connects the bedrooms with the rest of the house, this house was very open with wide

archways rather than doors between rooms that would provide ample accessibility for a wheelchair. Neither of the two bedrooms nor the bathroom would be easy to modify, but with the layout of the house and a large backyard, we were able to view this house as a "good start" that could be modified to suit our specific needs. We immediately began thinking about plans to add a new master suite out the back of the house, but first we had to purchase the property.

We had a longtime friend of the family, a realtor, inspect the house for us and give us an estimate of the worth of the house. Inspections verified that there were no inherent structural problems or other deal-breaking issues that we would want to know about in advance. We then got ready for the big day. Neither Geri nor I had previously purchased anything at a public sale, nor did I ever remember attending one. I guess you might say that we decided to start big.

Fortunately for us, my father, because of his profession, was accustomed to public sales and was there to help. On the day of the sale, in October 1996, I was very nervous. Once bidding started, I merely waited for my father to tap me on the shoulder as to when I should raise my hand. The auctioneer called out increasing values until just below our predetermined maximum and stopped. We had the high bid, or so we thought, and we waited. Going once... Going twice... Sold! And the auctioneer pointed to someone else on the other side of the yard! Our hearts stopped!

What happened was something my father told us he had never seen before in all his years as an attorney at public sales. The auctioneer made a *mistake* and completely missed my bid! My father responded promptly and pointed out to the auctioneer that the Conditions of Sale provide that if a dispute arises among bidders, the property will be immediately put up for rebidding. Others in attendance backed up our claim, and the auctioneer reopened bidding, giving us the high bid. The other bidder backed down. The house was ours!

Wow! I was shaking and relieved, in disbelief partially because we were buying a house, but mostly because of the way it happened. We were now ready to set a wedding date.

Within the next couple of days, we contacted two different contractors with whom we discussed our needs. We planned for an addition to be built out the back of the house that would be the master bedroom, bathroom, a walk-in closet, and an additional adjacent room that we affectionately labeled my "ready room," the name adopted from Captain Picard's ready room on *Star Trek-the Next Generation*. In this room, I would be able to get dressed, up into my chair, and prepared for the day, allowing Geri privacy to either get ready or sleep in, depending on the day's agenda. Each of the two contractors worked up plans and provided estimates. After making a final decision and choosing a contractor, we worked to finalize detailed plans, and the work began. Geri moved into the house right after settlement and lived in the house throughout the project.

The day the contractors broke through the dining room wall to open access between the addition and the existing house, they neglected to give Geri advance notice. She left her bedroom door open when she left for work that morning and came home to a layer of dust over everything. She needed to rewash everything in her closet.

I continued to commute to work from my parents' home in New Holland until after our wedding day, set for the following April 11.

Wedding and Honeymoon Preparations

Geri and I set the date and made plans to be wed on April 11, 1997 at Calvary Church, just outside of Lancaster, Pennsylvania. The house was under construction and would be ready for me to move in after the wedding. We worked out wedding details together, but the honeymoon was initially my responsibility.

When I was twelve years old, my family took a trip to Walt Disney World. Geri had never had that experience, and as a wedding gift, I wanted to give her that opportunity. Initially, I meant for it to be a surprise, but after purchasing park tickets and airfare, I decided that it would be better to work together in determining what we wanted to do while there.

Having the tickets and airfare already purchased, I sprang the surprise, and we worked together to plan for our time away. We made reservations for Prime Time Café at MGM (Sunday), Hoop-Dee-Doo Revue and Breakfast with Winnie the Pooh in the Crystal Palace in Magic Kingdom (Monday/Thursday), and Coral Reef Restaurant and Rose & Crown Pub in Epcot (Tuesday/Wednesday). The rest of the time, we would see what we could find. On Friday, we would go to Sea World.

Sadly, many of the details surrounding preparation for our wedding day and our honeymoon have departed from my memory. I don't know if I hit my head too many times over the years, if it's just a symptom of getting older, or if it's because it was more than twenty years ago, but I will detail what I can remember.

We chose our groomsmen and bridesmaids. My best man would be my brother, Mike, with Keith Youndt, one of my former gymnastics teammates, and Andy Heller, a friend from high school, as groomsmen. Geri chose Kerry Drout as her maid of honor, with Jen Smith and Sarah Ranck as bridesmaids.

The groomsmen and I picked out and sized our tuxedos from a rental in Ephrata, Pennsylvania, and followed that up with a trip to Dairy Queen. This ice cream trip was as much of a "bachelor party" as we would have as none of us gave it much thought at the time. I never did see the point in such parties.

We went through premarital counseling at our church with Pastor David Allen, who would also perform the wedding ceremony later that year.

We had finalized plans for the wedding and honeymoon, and we were ready to be wed on Friday night, April 11th. Our rehearsal dinner was held the night before the wedding at Lombardo's, an Italian restaurant in Lancaster.

On the night of our wedding, we all arrived at the church and prepared for the ceremony. The groomsmen and I, along with the bridesmaids, were standing up front as we and the rest of those in attendance awaited the entrance of the bride. When Geri saw me up front, she was so happy that she was in tears as she began walking up the aisle. Once up front, as prear-  ranged by the suggestion of Pastor Dave, she sat on a stool to exchange vows and rings in a way that enabled the two of us to be at eye level with one another. Everything during the ceremony proceeded as planned, and we became husband and wife, Mr. and Mrs. Timothy Weaver.

The only irregularity occurred with the lighting of the unity candle. The wick fell into the wax, and Pastor Dave lifted it up and out for us to light it.

At the conclusion, we decided to have some fun for the guests'  amusement. I turned toward the door, Geri hopped on the back of my chair, and I carried her out of the sanctuary. I sped down the aisle until Geri said to slow down for pictures on the way out. Nobody believed that we would exit in this fashion (not even Geri until we were doing it), and it garnered a few laughs. We headed out the back door and around the church to a lower-level multipurpose room.

For further amusement entering the reception, we had the bridesmaids push the groomsmen using wheelchairs, with Geri riding in on my lap.

Aside from the entrance, there was little that was in any way out of the ordinary at the reception. We had friends attending the wedding, from family, school, church, and the gymnastics community. A couple we knew from church provided the catering as a wedding gift. Unfortunately, health problems on the part of the caterers resulted in both sets of parents cleaning up after we had left the reception and gone home. Near the end of the evening, Geri's five-year-old nephew saw a little box on the wall with a red handle and white lettering that said: Pull. Everyone was suddenly alert when the fire alarm began blaring! Fortunately, most of the guests had already left. But interestingly, the fire company was unaware of the incident, the church finding out through this "accident" that nobody connected the fire alarms with the fire company.

Following the reception, Geri and I headed back to our new home where she had been living since the previous November. That night would be my first in the house that we had purchased together the year before.

Honeymoon

THE NEXT MORNING, my father drove us to Harrisburg Airport. This flight would be my first experience flying since my accident, and it would prove to be a memorable one. In the terminal, airline personnel lifted and strapped me onto a narrow chair that was capable of fitting down the aisle in the plane. It was not much more than a furniture dolly with a seat on it and was not very comfortable. Once in the plane, they belted me into the airplane seat with my wheelchair cushion as padding underneath me. When we arrived in Orlando, a wheelchair accessible van shuttled us from the airport to our room at Caribbean Beach Resort.

On Disney property we relied on Disney transportation for the week we were there. Walt Disney World had equipped a majority of their buses with wheelchair lifts. Amazing technologically, they did not utilize a separate entrance and weren't obstructive when not in use. The steps of the bus folded out to become the lift, making the lift itself virtually invisible when not in use.

As is always the case when I go away, the details and intricacies of my care do not change. I never get a vacation from my disability. We needed a room that was handicapped accessible. I had to arrange for a shower chair to be delivered to the resort for my use that week. I didn't want Geri to have to lift me into and out of bed morning and night, every single day, so I arranged for a Hoyer lift as well. What I didn't know up front was the size and layout of the bedroom or bathroom. It seems the world doesn't know much about what it means to be disabled, and everybody's definition of "handicapped accessible" is different.

Today, with the Internet, you can easily pull up images of the resorts. But in 1997, the Internet was still young, and this information was not readily available. The ADA (Americans with Disabilities Act) has brought about many needed changes in accessibility, but even today there are often struggles of which the majority of people have only a vague understanding.

The room was large enough to maneuver my wheelchair easily, but the bathroom, although accessible, was small. There was a roll-in shower that would accommodate me in my shower chair, but there wasn't much additional room for anyone else, in our case Geri, if bathing assistance was needed. Under normal circumstances, I had no problem showering myself. The shower chair we had rented, however, was not the same model I used at home, and I had difficulty with doing anything independently while sitting in it. By the end of my showers, Geri and I were both soaked.

As far as minimizing the work that Geri would have in lifting me that week, the Hoyer lift seemed like a good idea when I ordered it. But with neither of us being familiar with its operation, we opted against using it. We decided it would be more trouble than it was worth and we returned it after the first day.

The weather was less than desirable for our first day in Magic Kingdom. We spent a good bit of the day wearing bright yellow Mickey Mouse rain ponchos. Our trip took place before the institution of FastPasses, and instead, we were instructed to approach the ride attendants regarding my disability to bypass the lines. I think there was probably a lot of abuse of this privilege, and I believe that this is a large part of the motivation behind the FastPasses used now.

There were many attractions we could ride together, and a few I encouraged Geri to ride alone for the experience. It was nice that even on rides such as Dumbo the Flying Elephant, which was a ride Geri had wanted to ride from the time she was a little girl, and Space Mountain, she was able to jump to the front of the line so that I wouldn't have to wait for long time periods alone and without assistance. A random stranger was kind enough to snap a picture of Geri for me while she rode the carousel.

In the evening, we went to the Hoop-Dee-Doo-Revue dinner show for supper. At the time, we thought there was no other way to get there but by ferry. So we made our way to the dock only to find that it was not wheelchair accessible. So, in the dark and rain, I was lifted by four men, chair and all, onto the boat. No, it probably wasn't safe and probably wouldn't happen today because of liability concerns, but we got there and thoroughly enjoyed our dinner and show. We missed winning a door prize by one day when they asked for the newest newlyweds. There was one couple in the room that had been married Saturday, our wedding having been Friday night.

We spent two days at Epcot Center. While touring the World Showcase, we posed for pictures, Geri with Pooh and me with Goofy. The one with Goofy was a trip requirement, to go along with a portrait that my brother and I had taken on our family vacation when I was twelve.

Throughout the World Showcase, we enjoyed tastes of cultural entertainment and food, and decorating the park was a wide assortment of Disney character-shaped topiary. We also enjoyed a meal at the Coral Reef Restaurant overlooking the Seas Pavilion aquarium, and enjoyed spectacular fireworks displays at both Magic Kingdom and Epcot Center that week.

For the last full day of our trip, we had arranged for a wheelchair accessible van to pick us up for a day at Sea World. We enjoyed seeing Shamu, the walruses, sea lions, and all the other animals, and were surprised by the massive size of the walrus.

The following morning, we had to say goodbye to Florida, Walt Disney World, and the Caribbean Beach Resort. It was a fun week. We loved the environment and the great people with whom we interacted. Based on our experience that week, we felt that Walt Disney World was a very accommodating vacation spot for the disabled. Walt Disney World has since become a favorite family vacation destination.

We were picked up and driven back to the airport for our trip back to Pennsylvania and our new life as husband and wife.

Angus

Wᴇɴ I ᴡᴀs in college, a fellow student in my dorm had a service dog. At the time, I had not considered getting one myself. But not long after Geri and I were married, the question was raised about me having a dog for assistance with picking things up and possibly help sitting up in my chair if I fell over.

We visited Canine Partners for Life, located in Cochranville, Pennsylvania, to learn about service dogs. We went to the meeting with a list of questions such as: Is there a waiting list? What is the process and timeline for receiving a dog? And what is the expense? By the time we left, it was pretty clear in my mind that the cost was too high to consider moving forward at this time. Getting a dog would require me being off work for up to three weeks for a training period and service dog orientation. Canine Partners for Life was far enough away that I would not be able to stay home and commute for training. Living out of a hotel and arranging for my care during training time would not be easy. At this point in my life, I wasn't prepared or willing to give up that much of my time at work and home. The potential benefit was not worth the hassle. Had it been closer to home, allowing me to spend the nights in my bed and without needing to make alternate attendant care arrangements, I may have given it more consideration.

Several months later, we learned of a relatively new service dog organization, New Life Assistance Dogs, that had a short wait list, little upfront monetary investment, and the best part…they were located only about ten minutes from my home. We began to reassess the possibility of me getting a service dog. Boot camp would mean two weeks off work, but I could sleep in my bed and would not have to make any out-of-town attendant care arrangements. I submitted my application and waited for the start of boot camp.

In the meantime, we fenced in our backyard so that we could let a dog run free in the yard without concern. Our street was busy, and we were not going to allow any chance for our dog to run into traffic, no matter how well-trained it may be. An Amish neighbor was also breeding Dobermans and Rottweilers at the time. And while I know that many of these dogs are sweet and very friendly, these were not. These not-so-nice dogs occasionally got free, and we were not going to leave any provision for dog fights. We had considered invisible fencing, but this would only keep our dog in (maybe, but no guarantees) and make no provision for keeping the Amish farmer's dogs out.

The day finally arrived for me and a group of others who would also be receiving dogs. We were each paired with a dog and told that we may or may not finish the week with this particular dog. The idea behind group orientation was the identification of the best match of available dog and handler. Although she did not say it out loud, the trainer, Sabina, had a strong inclination that a black lab named Angus and I would be a perfect match. We were paired together and connected early. We began to bond as I learned the commands, and he learned to follow my instruction and trust my leadership. One day, I unexpectedly found Angus looking down at me after having leaped up, taking a seat on my lap.

But things were not always easy. Sabina warned us that the dogs would try to test us, and Angus was no exception. He did his best to frustrate me, most notably by tangling himself in the leash. While I worked hard to get him to untangle himself, Sabina encouraged me that Angus knew what to do and could get himself untangled if he wanted to. I liked this dog and was quickly growing attached, so I made up my mind that I was not going to allow myself to get frustrated, and this dog was not going to beat me.

My persistence paid off, and at one defining moment, something clicked between us, and we began working as a unit. It was then a matter of practice and taking our training to different environments and venues. We practiced loading and unloading from our vehicles, going to malls and stores, dealing with crowds, and eating in a restaurant. At the end of two weeks, Angus and I graduated from boot camp as a service dog team. From that point on, we went everywhere together and were rarely separated

Angus was a good dog and was a lot of fun. He came to us with a very unusual history. These service dogs begin their training very early. When they leave the litter, they go to a puppy home where they spend their first twelve to eighteen months and receive basic obedience training and socialization. In Angus' puppy home, he got into a bit of trouble. One day, while the puppy owner took a nap, he went in and out of the house and made a pile of rocks beside the couch. In another incident following a lot of commotion in the yard, Angus was found holding a rooster in his mouth, legs and beak sticking out forward. Surprisingly, neither the rooster nor Angus hurt the other in any way.

A most notable feature of Angus was a sneer that was very obvious when he would stare intently in your direction. When he was a puppy, he tried to eat a hollyhock plant. The fibers of the plant went up into the side of his face and caused an infection. The infection required surgery that resulted in minor nerve damage.

Finally, a trick that he learned at his puppy home was "So big." When he got excited, he would jump straight up into the air with all four legs and his back horizontal to the ground. The puppy home trainer taught him to do it on command when she said, "So Big" and raised her hands. Another trick that we taught him later on was "bang." When we said the word bang, he would lie down and roll over.

On a serious note, Angus was able to pick things up for me—things as small as a dime and as large as my lap desk and books. Papers and books didn't always fare well, but most of the time he was gentle with what he touched. The most frequently picked-up items were my cuffs, pencils, and the magnet I used to open and close my van. Angus also helped me clean up the house. He and I would go around and pick up his toys. He would put them on my lap, and I would carry them to his basket and drop them in. Angus enjoyed balls, Frisbees, and soft toys and was not destructive with anything.

For a while, Sabina made visits to my workplace to work on Angus' ability to help me sit up after falling forward in my chair, but this was something he was unable to do. We also worked with him to open some of the doors at work by pulling on ropes tied to the door handles. I frequently practiced with Angus by throwing papers and other things on the floor, so that when needed, he would be adept at helping me.

One thing that was difficult with Angus was getting his nails trimmed. It took up to five people to hold him still. I also struggled with him loading into my van. At the time, I drove a full-size Ford Econoline van. Shortly after Angus came into our lives, he slipped while entering and developed a fear of the high jump. As a solution, I lowered the lift halfway so that he could make two small leaps instead of one high one.

But taking into account both the good and the bad, we were a united team. We had a tight bond and lived up to the expectations of Sabina, who had trained Angus and knew we would be a good match.

Cameron

In 1999, HAVING been married for two years, Geri and I decided that we wanted to have a child. God had blessed us with a home and good jobs. Our marital relationship was strong, and we now wanted to extend that blessing to a new generation.

A friend with the same level of injury as mine, with his wife, successfully conceived and birthed a child. We briefly entertained the idea of natural childbirth, but in our hearts, we felt that God was leading us to adopt. We began the process by making inquiries at several adoption agencies and attending informational meetings. We applied to work with Adoptions from the Heart to find the right program and child and prayed that God would lead us to where we could fill the greatest need. We quickly discovered that, because of my disability, many programs and countries immediately disqualified us from consideration. Our only available options were to adopt from Eastern Europe or Southeast Asia. In the Eastern Europe program, we would choose an available child from a series of pictures. This choice, we believed, would be difficult. How could you pick one and not another? And on what basis is such a decision made? But we would never have to make that choice. After seeing a video of the orphanages in Southeast Asia, our hearts broke for these children, and we knew that this was where God was leading us. Adoptions from the Heart worked with a husband and wife from the United States who had a heart for Southeast Asian children, adopted a few themselves, and began working as facilitators with the Southeast Asia program. It eased my mind to know that Geri would not be traveling alone. Because of my disability, I was not able to make the trip to Southeast Asia. I felt much more comfortable knowing that there would be someone who knew the country and the program and would be guiding her every step of the way.

We began to work through the program requirements. There was a lot of paperwork, and the United States government, the Southeast Asian embassy, and our agency required fingerprints of each of us for background checks. Our caseworker told us up front that if we followed her instructions and finished the paperwork promptly, we could be traveling in about eight months. At the end of 1999, Geri left her job at Lancaster Labs to be a stay-at-home mom. She had worked in office services for a little under two years. By leaving, her schedule was freed-up, giving her time to handle the paperwork and get the house ready for a baby.

The paperwork was time-consuming, but getting my fingerprints was the most difficult of the program requirements. My fingers no longer straighten. Stiff, bent fingers are not usually a problem, and functionally it is advantageous, making it easier for me to pick things up. But it did make getting my fingerprints challenging. Because of my fingers, I was unable to use the electronic fingerprinting machines. So for me, we had to use ink. Some of my fingers were so difficult that I needed to have each finger printed individually using cadaver spoons.

Geri soon received word of her fingerprint approval. Mine, however, failed, meaning that I would have to travel back to Philadelphia to go through the whole process a second time. This time, a friend of mine drove me, saving Geri from having to drive into the city again. Two failed fingerprints would force a name-based background check, so I knew that there would not be a third attempt if the second failed.

After notarizing the completed paperwork, Geri drove the documents to the State Capitol in Harrisburg for state certification. We then mailed the paperwork overnight to a courier, who hand-delivered the packet to the embassy and waited for the completed translation. When we received the paperwork back, we submitted it to Adoptions from the Heart to forward it to Southeast Asia. And then we waited.

On March 2, 2000, we received an envelope in the mail. Geri called me and said that she was on her way to Lancaster Labs. We met in the lobby and opened the package together. Inside was a referral and picture for a four-month-old Southeast Asian boy.

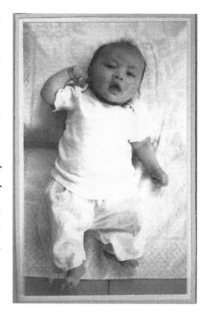

Because of the regularity of the program, there were groups of adoptive parents traveling every month or two. That made it easy to limit the visits by any one family to one trip. Each group would sign the acceptance, or intent to adopt, paperwork for the following group's adoptions. So our little boy was signed for shortly after we received the packet in the mail. We then awaited word on the scheduling of Geri's flight to Southeast Asia.

About a week later, we received our flight plan. Then, three years after we were married, Geri and I spent our third anniversary apart. We were culminating the eight-month process of adopting a five-month-old boy from Southeast Asia. Geri took along Kerry Drout, who had been her maid of honor, for companionship and assistance during the trip. Once they returned to Pennsylvania, we formally adopted him into our family and gave him the name Cameron. The agency warned us that children from Southeast Asia were often undernourished, small, and likely developmentally delayed when compared with children born in the United States. We found, however, that Cameron would very quickly overcome any developmental deficiencies that may have been present at the time of adoption. Cameron was the latest and thus far greatest blessing that God had given us in our marriage.

Connor

ABOUT A YEAR after Cameron's adoption, we decided to get a second dog. Cameron missed Angus while I had him at work, so we got a chocolate Lab puppy we named Annabelle. We only had her for a year, however. She began showing signs of jealousy whenever Angus was getting the attention. She reacted by trying to chew on his neck. She was also showing aggression toward Cameron and had broken the skin on Geri's hand.

In 2001, we decided that Cameron needed a little brother. We were concerned about bringing a new baby into the house when Annabelle was already manifesting aggressive behavior. We decided that she needed a new home, one in which she would not have competition from other dogs or children. Because she was a part of our family, we wanted to make sure that she would go to a good home. We were sad about saying goodbye, but Annabelle lived a full and enjoyable life. She was spoiled by a gentleman who gave her all the attention she needed.

We went back to Adoptions from the Heart and began the process to return to Southeast Asia. We would use the same agency, the same program, and the same facilitators, but this time it would take a little bit longer. We went through the same paperwork, with the same notarization, state certification, and translation requirements. We both needed new background checks, meaning repeated fingerprinting. And yes, I had to do it twice again.

The most significant difference this time was the need for Geri to make two trips to Southeast Asia. No longer were others allowed to sign for the child that someone else would be adopting. For Cameron's adoption, we also did not specify gender when requesting a child. We decided to leave it in God's hands and let God, through the country, choose for us. That said, our caseworker told us that we would likely adopt a boy because most people request girls. This time, though, we specifically asked for a boy so that he could share a room with Cameron. And so we finished our paperwork, had it delivered to Adoptions from the Heart to send to Southeast Asia, and waited.

On May 22, we received an envelope in the mail containing information about our second little boy. We then awaited flight information for the two trips that Geri would be taking.

On June 6, Geri flew to Southeast Asia for the first trip, June 6–12. In Southeast Asia, she was handed our little boy, asked to inspect him, and sign an acceptance form for the child. The hard part about this trip was that Geri could hold the child for one hour and then had to give him back and leave the country. The next month was a very long month as we awaited her second trip date.

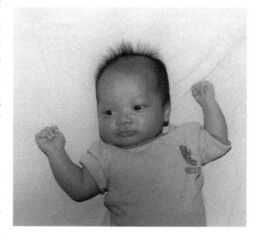

But on July 28, 2002, Geri took off for Southeast Asia, July 28–Aug 7. This time, George and Patty Hauber went along to help Geri. Many years earlier, the Haubers had adopted Suzanne, who had been born in Southeast Asia, not far from the orphanage where our boys had lived. They joined Geri to help, but also, with Suzanne, to visit and tour the orphanage and the surrounding area in Southeast Asia where she was born.

There was a bit more uncertainty and urgency during this trip than the one two years earlier when we adopted Cameron. There were rumors that the program was shutting down, partially due to issues between the two countries, but primarily because the international adoption agreement between the United States and Southeast Asia was expiring. Had the program shut down while they were in Southeast Asia, Geri would have come home empty-handed. But the facilitators were wise to what was happening. It was so close, however, that the facilitators adjusted the schedule and hustled Geri and other prospective parents to the DMV to stay ahead of the looming dispatch that we learned was also on its way to the DMV to stop any further approvals. They made it in time, and Cameron's younger brother was soon in hand and ready for the trip back to Pennsylvania. Once they returned to the States, we adopted Connor into the family.

Raising Boys

RAISING CHILDREN IS never easy, but being disabled makes it even more difficult. Especially when the boys were babies and toddlers, most of the responsibility fell on Geri. I could not change diapers, get them dressed, or feed them. I could try to occupy their attention and keep an eye on them, but couldn't do much if they got into trouble.

But as they grew, I became more involved in their lives. I couldn't do everything dads typically do with boys. I couldn't play ball or get down on the floor with them to wrestle or roughhouse. I couldn't work with my hands or tools to build things with them, but I could give them my time and attention. In good weather, I spent hours outside with the boys, pushing them on swings or racing my wheelchair around and around the backyard with one or both of them on my lap, standing on the back of my chair, or riding behind me in a wagon or "big red car." The big red car was a Little Tykes Cozy Coupe that we found at a yard sale, but it got lots of mileage as I hooked Angus' leash around the front post and pulled it all over our backyard. The boys loved it!

I took them on walks around the neighborhood, with Angus leashed beside me and the wagon behind. When the boys got older, they rode bikes at the church parking lot down the street from our house.

A game we enjoyed indoors when the boys were young we called "whee!" The boys and I raced in circles through our bedroom, bathroom, ready room, and closet. The boys usually pushed trucks around the loop, and I either led the way or followed, depending on how you look at it. At times, we got going quite fast. Most of the time I navigated well, but doorframes occasionally got scraped. While I'm not excited to admit it, on one occasion, I did misjudge a turn, cracked the doorframe, and ripped the bathroom door off its hinges.

The boys' favorite toys included Legos, puzzles, and Thomas the Tank Engine wooden tracks. I couldn't physically put things together,

but the boys were open to suggestions and verbal direction as they acted as my hands to implement ideas and build for me. My guidance helped to spur their imaginations, and we worked together to create. Railway track layouts sometimes encompassed a large portion of our living room and dining room.

I introduced the boys to the computer when they were young. They sat on my lap and played games that were appropriate for their ages. Even while young, Cameron soon began programming and graphical development. He researched and built computers for both himself and Connor when he was thirteen. We also enrolled the boys in gymnastics classes when they were young, and they enjoyed recreational activities at the gym for which I had competed. They took classes, one day a week, for many years.

Between my need for care and my lack of ability to help with the boys care, we didn't go on many vacations. We went to Joni and Friends Family Retreat for one year with both boys in 2003 but then went on no overnight trips until 2011, when friends invited us to join them for a weekend at the beach. We enjoyed day-trips to zoos, aquariums, and other local attractions, but nothing that required an overnight stay. In 2016, some friends invited us to join them for a trip to Walt Disney World, which we eagerly accepted. The following year, we spent a week at Ocean City, New Jersey with my parents. At that point, the boys were old enough to help with some of my care, enabling us to go to more places.

By the time the boys finished first and third grade, respectively, we decided to pull them from public school. We had problems with the public school system and decided that homeschooling them was the best option for our family. We researched and purchased curriculum, joined a co-op, and prepared for our new adventure.

Geri did most of the teaching and coordinated the boys work. I helped initially with math oversight and correction, but once we switched to Teaching Textbooks, a computer-based program with video instruction, the boys were mostly independent in their studies. We enjoyed the flexibility homeschooling provided for our family and agree, looking back, that we made the right decision. Bible was included with each year's curriculum, and we could teach subject matter in history and science from a biblical perspective.

We encouraged the boys to find things that they enjoyed as goals for future employment. Cameron's natural giftedness with computers made his decision easy, and by the time he graduated, he was already doing freelance development online. Connor had a much more difficult time identifying a goal, and at the time of this writing, he is unsure of his future pursuits. He is naturally gifted musically and enjoys playing keyboard and guitar. He likes to cook but is not sure that he wants to be a chef. To him, music and cooking are simply hobbies. We are working with him to develop his educational objectives, but with a couple of years left before he graduates, he still has time to decide.

While the boys were in grade school, I volunteered at church in the fourth grade and colead a small group for both Cameron and Connor as they reached that grade. I enjoyed the opportunity to teach and share of myself what God had given to me. Until the boys were in their teens, each day typically ended with Geri reading to them from one or more books, after which I read from the Bible and frequently a devotional. Biblical teaching and prayer were an essential part of each day. Faith discussions were commonplace, and both boys made professions of faith when they were young.

Watching our sons mature as they grew has been a God-given blessing. I have emphasized to them the importance of living for God and have encouraged them to develop their relationship with Jesus. I hope and pray that they have taken my teaching to heart and continue to live in faith when I am no longer a part of their lives.

Problems with Angus

FROM THE TIME that Angus came into our family, he struggled with ear infections. No matter what we did, we couldn't keep his right ear clean. We eventually opted to have his ear canal and inner ear surgically removed. The veterinarian told us that he was most likely already deaf in the ear and that he would suffer less without it. Following surgery, the ear flap was still in place, but it covered only a scar where his ear had once been. Before long, he was back at work with me and by my side.

Angus also suffered seizures that required medication for epilepsy. Later in life, he developed hypothyroidism. We noticed that he started gaining weight uncontrollably. On a visit to United Disabilities Services (UDS), the trainer looked at him and said, "Angus, you're a coffee table!" With medication and a controlled diet, we were able to keep these conditions mostly under control.

In 2004, I was sitting at the dining room table, Angus sitting to my left, and the front door to my right. I was petting him and had my hand in his collar when the doorbell rang. Angus ran to the door barking and yanked my arm behind the back of my chair. I looked at Geri, and my face turned pale. With my left arm dangling by my side, all I could say was: "I think Angus broke my arm."

Geri called her parents to watch the boys, and then called the ambulance. She wrapped my arm in an ace bandage to stabilize it. In the ER, X-rays revealed a spiral fracture. We were amazed after seeing it that the bone didn't break through my skin, Geri's bandaging doing a great job keeping my arm secure. We met with an orthopedic surgeon, who told us that the only viable option was to repair my arm surgically with a metal bar and screws.

With my limited feeling and mobility and the severity of the break, casting my arm would have put me at risk for pressure related sores. Working around a cast would have also complicated my care and made transfers between bed and wheelchair more difficult. A full arm cast would have prevented me from controlling my wheelchair, leaving me even more dependent on others than I already was. I would have required someone with me, all day, every day, most likely precluding me from returning to work until fully healed. Complete recovery without surgery would take at least eight to twelve weeks. The projected recovery time following surgery was much less and would allow me to resume a semblance of my normal daily activities much sooner. I was admitted to the hospital and awaited surgery.

The operation was successful, but the adventure had only just begun. This type of procedure would typically be outpatient, but being a quadriplegic is anything but ordinary. We needed to be sure that my care was in place to handle my new and hopefully temporary limitations and restrictions. Before going home, my attendants came into the hospital for instructions in moving me. I do stand pivot transfers between bed and wheelchair. Transferring requires me, to the best of my ability, wrapping my arms around the shoulders of the person moving me, and holding on. Until my arm had time to heal, I would have my arm in a sling during transfers, leaving me only one arm to hold on with.

After spending eight days in the hospital, I returned home. I still had limitations on how much I could do with the arm, however, and would for quite some time. For transfers, and overnight, I kept my arm in a sling. As I could not drive, I was reliant on Geri for transportation, and while hopeful, was not sure that I would be able to drive ever again. For the first couple of weeks at work, I could only type using one hand and was very glad that I had Dragon Naturally Speaking™ installed, enabling me to type by dictation. I was accustomed to hooking one or the other arm around the handles of my chair for support and balance, but would be unable to do so now or possibly ever again. Activities requiring stabilization, such as eating, were more difficult. For a while, I could not even pick up my mug to drink, using straws instead. It took months of patience, but eventually, everything returned to normal. I was able to drive again, making Geri's life easier, and I could use both arms equally, including hooking and support, with no restrictions.

Angus was distraught while I was in the hospital, it being the first time that he was apart from me for more than a day since we graduated from boot camp. Geri did bring him into the hospital to see me, but then he went home without me. After getting out of the hospital, we began to think that we should start leaving Angus at home on an increasing basis. We realized that at some point he would need to retire and stay home permanently.

We quickly discovered that he was an emotional wreck when left alone. He would empty the trash can and chew things up. On one occasion he even peed on some of the boys coloring books and crayons. We purchased a crate for him for when he was home alone. He hated it, and we had difficulty getting him to go in. We ended up tying a leash to a dresser next to his bed to confine him.

As the years went by, Angus began to wear out more quickly, and he was slower to get up. He also developed sores on the "elbow" areas of his front legs. We knew that he would soon need to retire. Doing this, however, would not be straight forward. Ideally, he would retire in our home and live out the remainder of his days with us, but that would require that he become accustomed to being left home alone. The other option would be for him to retire in a home with a family or individual who could provide more consistent, daily, round-the-clock companionship, but that would mean the breakup of a nine-year team and relationship in which I was his nearly constant companion. We were very concerned that he would not take that separation well.

The sores on his legs kept getting worse and became infected. The vet said our best option at this point was surgery. With that choice before us, we made the difficult decision to not put an 11-year-old dog through anesthesia and surgery. He was growing old and already dealing with epilepsy, hypothyroidism, and separation anxiety. With retirement near and no good options for his mental and emotional well-being, we decided that it was time to say goodbye. Before Angus and I left work for the last time that morning, the trainer for UDS Service Dogs came to say good-bye, bringing along a container of chicken nuggets to share with Angus. We then met up with Geri at home. The boys said good-bye in our driveway, and Geri and I took Angus to the vet, where he drifted peacefully off to sleep for the last time. It was probably the hardest thing I have ever done.

It felt strange leaving the vet without him, and for a long time, I felt like I was missing a part of myself. When preparing to move my chair, I still looked for him to make sure that I wasn't going to run over his paws. It was a difficult adjustment, but eventually, we all moved on.

Adoption Journey—Southeast Asia and Foster Care

AFTER GERI CAME home with Connor in 2002, we discussed the possibility of going back to Southeast Asia again. Geri had envisioned us with three children, and we decided that we would like to try and make this happen. But for the time being, our desires were on hold, the program shut down for contract renegotiation.

A couple of years later, the United States and Southeast Asia agreed on a new contract, the program reopened, and Adoptions from the Heart announced that they were once again accepting applications for adoptions from Southeast Asia. We submitted our application and worked through the paperwork and fingerprinting for the third time. We completed our paperwork and had it notarized, state certified, and translated in much the same way as with our previous adoptions.

We submitted our completed paperwork to Adoptions from the Heart to mail to Southeast Asia, and we waited,…and waited,…for 18 long months. Some of the paperwork expired after one year, and because of the length of time we were waiting, we had to redo the forms. Then the relations between the United States and Southeast Asia fell apart, and the program closed again, and with it, our hopes for a third Southeast Asian adoption were all but gone.

We learned about and applied to adopt from Southeast Asia through a different program with the Pearl S. Buck Foundation. We attended all the required orientation and training classes and began working through the paperwork for adoption. We found a young girl who was available to adopt, submitted our autobiographies, and received preliminary approval from the embassy. As a family, we were excited about the possibility of bringing this young girl into our home.

A couple of weeks later, our caseworker informed us that the embassy had rescinded their initial approval and needed more information to make a final decision. She told us that approval was still possible but not guaranteed because of my disability. The embassy wouldn't decide until we had completed and submitted our dossier, along with any non-refundable country program fees. Only then would we get an answer, and there were no guarantees it would be favorable. We decided that the investment risk, both monetarily and emotionally, was too high after having just come off of one failed adoption. While we still desired to expand our family, the overseas options were disappearing. Our preference for another adoption was Southeast Asia, but doors were closing, and more and more, it seemed that that was not God's plan for our family at this time.

When our attempts to adopt from Southeast Asia failed, we turned to the foster care system locally. Over several years, we were approved with two different foster care agencies and accepted a couple of placements, but none resulted in adoption. We concluded that God meant for our family to be just the four of us, at least at this stage in our lives. The boys were getting older, and our focus needed to be on them. Geri and I still entertain the idea of foster care sometime in the future, but not while the boys are still living at home.

Riley, Concussions, and Raven

AFTER ANGUS DIED, I had no interest in getting another dog, much less a service dog. A couple of years later, however, after receiving encouragement and support from family and friends, I signed up with UDS Service Dogs once again. The trainers matched me with a yellow Labrador Retriever named Riley. There was no boot camp or official graduation this time. Riley came home with us almost immediately, and I worked with the trainers individually in my home and work environment rather than in group training at the UDS facility.

It soon became apparent that Riley had a barking problem; he routinely barked at people who he assessed to be a threat to me, and I had a difficult time breaking him of this behavior. For two years I worked with Riley, and with the trainers' assistance, we tried everything that we could think of to help him. During most of those two years, I took Riley nowhere outside of the house but to work. Although I tried initially to take him everywhere, I limited him to work and church after recognizing his problems. Because he barked during services and Wednesday night meals, I soon stopped taking him to church as well. We were hesitant to take him to any stores or restaurants because inevitably he would bark and lunge at someone passing by our table. We couldn't relax with him out in public, as I always had to be on guard, keeping an eye out for any possible people or situations that he might deem a threat. Perhaps my demeanor and alertness contributed to the problem, but regardless, we were unable to make it work for him as a service dog.

While my tenacity worked with Angus, it failed to bring satisfactory results with Riley. The family, especially the boys and I, had gotten quite attached to him, nonetheless, and it would have been difficult to return him to UDS after two years as a member of our family. So we decided to keep him at home, more as a family pet than a service dog, and he stopped going to work with me from that point on. We later learned that service dogs occasionally develop a hypersensitivity to the needs and well-being of their owners, and this was most likely the case with Riley. I couldn't even sneeze without him panicking. Although he stopped going to work with me, he still picked things up at home for me as needed.

Less than a year after receiving Riley, we decided to add a second dog to our family as a family pet. At the time, Riley was still going with me to work, and Geri and the boys wanted a dog at home during the day. One of the trainers with UDS service dogs was breeding Labrador Retrievers, and Geri took the boys to see the puppies after they were born. Connor fell in love with one, the runt of the litter. He held the dog almost the whole time they were there, and before it was time to leave, he said: "I'm not leaving here without her." That was not going to happen, as it was too early for the puppies to leave the litter, but they had set their hearts on bringing this puppy home a couple of weeks later.

Raven was a well-behaved dog right from the beginning; she was easy to train and had a great disposition. Her health, on the other hand, was an issue. She was sick for a while after we got her, and we had trouble finding food she would eat. Eventually, her health improved, but when she was two years-old, she woke up one morning and would not put weight on her back left leg. During visits to several veterinary facilities including multiple X-rays, we learned that she had injured her left knee while compensating for pain in an ill-formed right hip. Considering she was only two years-old, we opted to repair her knee surgically. Following surgery, the veterinarian recommended that she have a full hip replacement to prevent future complications.

Especially at the time, we were not inclined to spend $7000 on another surgery for a dog. The first surgery and previous health concerns had already cost us more than $5000. Had it not been for recent events surrounding Connor, however, we may not have even done this much.

The previous October 2012, Connor slipped on our garage floor while running out of the rain and landed flat on his back. His leg jammed under the riding mower, and his head hit the floor. We didn't know much about concussions, and initial signs of a concussion were negative. Our primary concern was the pain in his hip. Over the next four months, Connor dealt with numerous stomach issues including pain almost every time he ate, resulting in many doctor visits and testing to identify the cause. In February 2013, he slipped again running into the garage and was this time diagnosed with a concussion. As we dealt with concussion symptoms and recovery, we learned that Connor's stomach issues were very likely a concussion symptom, meaning that he also suffered a concussion in October. We learned that two concussions only four months apart could have killed him. We were all relieved that he was alive.

Connor missed nearly a year of school following his injury and was developmentally and emotionally delayed. He had numerous MRIs, X-rays, CAT scans, and visits with doctors and concussion specialists to diagnose and manage symptoms. He dealt with headaches, memory loss, anger, and confusion for a long time, and only four to five years later was he able to live a "normal" life and keep up with schoolwork. Even now, though, he still struggles with sleep issues and occasional headaches.

Raven's knee injury and subsequent surgery occurred not long after Connor's concussions. The last thing we wanted to do was add the loss of his dog to the list of physical and emotional trials he was already enduring. And so we made it clear to him that he was more important than the money that we were spending to make his dog better.

Although we tried numerous other pets in addition to our dogs over the years, our allergies prevented us from keeping any of them. Riley passed away in December 2018 at the age of eleven, and we decided that Raven was the last pet we would own. Dealing with our dogs' end of life situations is difficult, and our lives at this point require flexibility without pets.

A Relationship with Jesus

As of the date of this writing, it has been sixteen years since we adopted Connor. I continue to work at Lancaster Laboratories, now owned by Eurofins Scientific LLC, and Geri remains in the home as a stay-at-home mom. In 2010, we traded in my Ford Econoline van for a new 2010 Honda Odyssey. I drove that van for six years. As a result of a head-on collision caused by my falling asleep at the wheel on a trip home from Hershey Medical Center in December 2016, the Honda was a total loss. Everyone survived the crash, but I spent ten days, including Christmas day, in the hospital following surgery to repair my leg. I had broken all three bones in my right leg and required rods and pins to hold everything together. I had also fractured a rib and several vertebrae and punctured a lung that precipitated the need for a breathing tube while the lung healed. I nearly died that week because of complications with my lungs. One night I was unable to breathe, and I woke up to the respiratory therapist suctioning fluid out of my lungs, arguably the most unpleasant experience of my life. Had the therapist not acted promptly, I don't know that I would have lived through the night. By God's grace, I am alive, but I have not driven since. While I hope to someday get a new van I can drive, it is unlikely.

My life has not been easy, and I have dealt with many trials over the years. Recurrent urinary tract infections, several landing me in the hospital, have been a major concern and have precipitated many changes in bladder management. Aside from my physical limitations, one of my continuous difficulties has been finding consistent, reliable attendant care. While I understand that it is usually unavoidable, it's frustrating when an attendant calls or texts in the morning and I am left lying in bed scrambling to find help with getting up. While my family is available to help in an emergency, I have tried to keep my family life and attendant care as separate as possible. I learned before getting married that there are more than enough other stresses in a marital relationship, and I have done my best to keep Geri from having to do my care. If I do not have a scheduled attendant for a night or know in advance that I have no one for the following morning, I usually choose to sleep sitting up in my chair rather than to have Geri put me into bed and get me up. To help out when short on paid care-givers, I've also had friends who have come to my aid. My care is not difficult and requires no nursing background, but finding reliable care has proven to be a never-ending effort. Living with a disability such as mine is an ongoing struggle, but God has been with me the entire way. The events of my life are not what I would have chosen, but God is in control of all things and works all things, good and bad, for the good of those who love Him and are called according to His purpose (Romans 8:28–29).

Throughout my lifetime, I have struggled with physical limitations and trials, but God has wonderfully blessed me with a loving wife and two amazing sons. He has given us a home and a job I enjoy with which I can support a family. Regardless of our future, whether difficult or easy. I know that God will continue to watch over us. I know that our time on this earth is only temporary, with the reality of an eternal heavenly future waiting to come.

But not everyone will experience this heavenly future. While it is a gift given freely by the grace of God, it is only available because of the saving work of Jesus Christ on the cross. Only those who humbly acknowledge their complete inability to contribute in any way to their salvation and trust in Jesus Christ alone will be saved. It does not matter if you have attended church your entire life. It does not matter how good you try to be, how much you serve others, or how much money you give to God's work.

To think that we can do anything to add to what Jesus has already done is to say that Jesus' death and resurrection to break the power of sin and death was not enough.

Thanks to God, it was enough, and we can reap the benefits of that sacrifice for the forgiveness of our sins. If you have never humbled yourself before God and have never acknowledged that Jesus is your only hope for salvation, don't wait another day. We don't know what each day holds in store for us. We may not have another day or even another hour. Below is a prayer that was written by John Barnett that explains how you can freely receive God's gift of salvation. You can secure your eternal future by praying this prayer from your heart to God:

> *Dear God, I know that I am a sinner and there is nothing that I can do to save myself. I confess my complete helplessness to forgive my own sin or to work my way to heaven. At this moment, I trust Christ alone as the One who bore my sin when He died on the cross. I believe that He did all that will ever be necessary for me to stand in your holy presence. I thank you that Christ was raised from the dead as a guarantee of my own resurrection. As best as I can, I now transfer my trust to Him. I am grateful that He has promised to receive me despite my many sins and failures. Father, I take you at your word. I thank you that I can face death now that you are my Savior. Thank you for the assurance that you will walk with me through the deep valley. Thank you for hearing this prayer. In Jesus' Name, Amen.*

If you have just prayed this prayer and believe from your heart what you have prayed, your eternal future is secured by the promise of God through the death and resurrection of Jesus. But it is not the words or the prayer that save you as if this were some magic spell or powerful mantra, but the underlying belief spurred by a changed heart that will ultimately result in life change that glorifies God. The only requirement for salvation is to believe that Jesus is your sole and complete source of salvation and life.

If you have never felt the personal presence of Jesus in your life, I urge you to not worry. Although many Christians have "close to God" experiences, salvation is not about feelings but only the choice to believe. Regardless of whether or not you feel it, God is alive and well, and the Bible is living and active. God's timing is not always our timing, and He may not choose to reveal Himself in the way we think He should.

For me, a relationship with Jesus began with an understanding of who I was and what my eternal destination would be apart from Christ. That left me with a desire to increase my knowledge and understanding of God, who made my salvation possible. An understanding of what Jesus endured overflowed in a torrent of gratitude that guides me when I decide to sacrifice a part of myself for Him. Knowing that God is in complete control of everything and that there are no coincidences enables me to see the events in my life as God's handiwork. I can see even the little things in life that are frequently claimed as chance happenings to be God-ordained incidents, or "goincidences," a phrase I have coined to describe my understanding of life events. When such an incident occurs, I read something in Scripture, or I listen to a message from God's Word, I can hear God speaking into my life.

Through prayer, I talk to God, anticipating an answer. Responses are not usually instantaneous, not always positive, and frequently involve waiting. But I know that God hears every prayer, and I trust Him even when I don't receive a direct response. While silence may be God saying, "No," He could just be telling me to "Wait." Regardless, God has shown me through the events of my life that He is present in the world and my life and that He loves me. A relationship is available to you as well. Ask God to come into your life and make Himself real to you.

But like any relationship, intimacy won't be instantaneous. While obtaining salvation requires only that you accept Jesus' sacrificial gift in redemption of your sin, developing a deep, personal relationship with your Savior takes time and effort. It doesn't do any good to say that you want a relationship with your neighbor and then never pick up the phone or walk next door. In the same way, a relationship with Jesus won't develop and grow if you aren't consistently in God's Word and fellowshipping with other believers. God lives in and through His people. Your relationship will stagnate if you aren't spending time in prayer and looking at the world through the lens of Scripture. In my life, I hardly recognized it happening, but over years of going to church and spending time in God's Word, my association and connection with Jesus have strengthened. Looking back over my life, I can now see a back and forth relationship developing as I have grown to know and love Him more. It is more than an emotional habit to which I have become accustomed. The Bible makes sense intellectually and agrees with history, archaeology, and science.

If you build your worldview starting with God's Word and look at your life with the understanding that God is working in everything happening around you, you will be able to pray more effectively and see God working more and more. God does not promise that life will be easy, but states that "in this world you will have tribulation" (John 16:33). The verse continues though, declaring that we should "take heart" because He has "overcome the world." As I have been thinking back over my life, God brought to mind a song I loved while growing up entitled *Turn Your Eyes Upon Jesus* by Helen Howarth Lemmel.

> O soul, are you weary and troubled?
> No light in the darkness you see?
> There's light for a look at the Savior,
> And life more abundant and free.
>
> ---
>
> (chorus) Turn your eyes upon Jesus,
> Look full in His wonderful face,
> And the things of earth will grow strangely dim,
> In the light of His glory and grace.
>
> ---

Through death into life everlasting
He passed, and we follow Him there;
O'er us sin no more hath dominion
For more than conqu'rors we are!

His Word shall not fail you, He promised;
Believe Him and all will be well;
Then go to a world that is dying,
His perfect salvation to tell!

If you have prayed the prayer above, take heart; God has your future in his hands and your ultimate good in mind, no matter what may happen in your life. Remember that life is much more than the here and now. It is the plan of God encompassing all time, space, and matter, and culminating in a future eternal reality. Live now with eternity in view and remember that you are not alone. If you are not attending a Bible-believing church, make every effort to find a church you can connect with that can help you grow in your new-found faith and cultivate your relationship with Jesus.

Can I Be Certain of My Salvation?

Aм I truly saved, or am I deceiving myself and living a façade? That is a question that was recently posed to me. You may have wondered this as well, whether you have been a Christian for many years or if you have just come to a saving knowledge of Jesus. How can you truly know? Or can you? Is it even possible?

Before I go any further, let me define what I'm referring to when I use the word "saved." This word is used with the understanding that people are inherently sinful, having violated God's law, with the consequence of being eternally separated from God. What this means is that when life on earth comes to an end, mankind is destined to an eternity in hell and eternal separation from God.

So when I use the word saved, I am talking of being saved from eternal damnation, and rescued to an eternal life free of suffering and pain in the presence of a holy, righteous, good, and loving God. I am not referring to salvation from pain and suffering during our earthly lives just as Jesus Himself was not spared the pain, humility, and suffering of life on earth. During His ministry, He shared with His disciples that "in this world you will have tribulation, but take heart, I have overcome the world (John 16:33)." That is not to say that He will not remove some of our sufferings from time to time, and He does heal certain individuals as part of His all-encompassing purpose and plan. But in many cases, He uses our suffering and our trials to advance His plans and to test and strengthen our faith.

So is it, then, possible to know with certainty whether or not your salvation is real? This is a difficult question to answer because the people who are most likely asking are either unsaved or are young in their faith and experiencing doubt over their eternal security in Christ as a result of recent conversion. They may not have experienced any period of time in which their faith has been tested, tried, and prevailed, and thus have not seen their own faith produce tangible evidence, yet. This is what Jesus talks about in the parable of the wheat and the tares (Matthew 13:24–30).

Initially, it is impossible to tell the difference between the wheat, representing true followers of Jesus having real, lasting, abiding faith, and the tares, who look like followers of Jesus on the outside, but whose faith is not real and will not last when the novelty wears off or is choked away by the cares or trials of the world.

Where does real, abiding faith come from? It comes from God, who prepares a person's heart for reception of the gospel message and plants the seed of faith. Without God's intervention into a person's life, each individual will live out his or her life with the objective of maximizing personal gain and selfish ambition, claiming freedom of will and free choice, yet all the while remaining a slave to sin and separated from God.

The first evidence of one's faith is in his or her ability to comprehend the salvation message and accept the truth outlined in God's Word, internalizing the gospel message and calling out to Jesus as Lord and Savior. It's not about us and a decision on our part to have faith. We cannot choose to believe unless God has first opened our hearts to the truth. The signs of true faith, given by God, and beginning with a decision to act on the revelation that God gives us will manifest themselves in our lives over time. Once God, through the Spirit, opens a person's heart to the person of Jesus and begins the faith journey, it is at that point that the necessary decision on the part of the individual to put one's complete faith and trust in Jesus as Lord and Savior becomes possible.

At first, it is impossible to tell if one's calling out to Jesus is initiated by true, lasting faith, or is merely a human effort at self-preservation in order to avoid the impending horror of an eternity in hell. The sincerity of the action will only become apparent over time as God works in the life of the new believer and the results of the conversion become visible to those around. If the action was one of self-preservation only, without the foundation of God-given faith, that person will not stay true to their confession. How long this takes for the visible manifestation of true faith to appear will be different from person to person, but no man can stay true to God's Word and remain faithful to God on his own. In the parable of the sower (Matthew 13:3–23), Jesus described four different scenarios in which the seed of God's Word was spread. In each of the first three scenarios, the individual receiving the message of salvation did not have a heart that was prepared by God, conditioned to enable faith to grow, and the seed never took root. In only one of the four scenarios did the seed of faith sprout and develop roots that were able to sustain growth in our world's conditions. Even though the seeds of faith, the reality of God, and the message of salvation are liberally scattered all over the world, not all hearts are prepared, conditioned, and able to provide the environment necessary for the seed of faith to germinate and grow.

But if a person's faith is real, roots will be spread that will never die. This is guaranteed because the source of nutrients supporting growth is not in the individual person or in anything of this world, but God alone and not dependent on any situations or circumstances that this world provides. And like Paul, we can be confident that once God has begun a good work in our lives, it will be carried through to completion (Philippians 1:6). If a person's faith is real, that person's life will begin to manifest and show forth what in Scripture is called the "fruit of the Spirit." And in increasing measure, a follower of Jesus will be characterized by a life of love, joy, peace, patience, kindness, goodness, faithfulness, gentleness, and self-control. Such an individual would love God's Word, take pleasure in seeking to obey God's commandments, and seek out and enjoy the company of fellow believers. Things of this world would naturally take on lesser importance over time than those things that have bearing on eternity.

Each individual is different, however, with some bearing much fruit and others only a little. The rate of change varies from believer to believer, and also throughout the life of an individual believer. We undoubtedly go through periods of time in which we grow at a faster rate than others. There may also be times when a believer is drawn to things of this world, diverting his or her focus from God and His word, and hiding their new character in Christ. But if such an individual's faith is real, the trend over time will be toward increasing Christlikeness.

God's Word describes what a true follower of Jesus looks like. If an individual spends time in God's Word, that person can increasingly see how their life compares to the portrait that God paints. Over time, as a believer becomes more and more familiar with God's Word and more attuned to the changes that are taking place in his or her life, that individual can validly know whether he or she is truly saved.

> If we receive the testimony of men, the testimony of God is greater, for this is the testimony of God that he has borne concerning his Son. Whoever believes in the Son of God has the testimony in himself. Whoever does not believe God has made him a liar, because he has not believed in the testimony that God has borne concerning his Son. And this is the testimony, that God gave us eternal life, and this life is in his Son.
>
> Whoever has the Son has life; whoever does not have the Son of God does not have life. I write these things to you who believe in the name of the Son of God that you may know that you have eternal life. (1 John 5:9–13)

So am I truly saved or am I living a façade? From what I have learned from God's Word and the things that I've seen in the way He has worked in my life, orchestrating everything and revealing Himself to me through His creation, His Word, and the circumstances and events of my life, I am confident in the faith that God has given me. I do not boast in and of myself and my accomplishments, but only Christ, who is the source of my salvation, the author of my life, my strength, my all. It is only through Christ that I am who I am and where I am today, and I owe everything to Him. To God alone be praise and glory!

You as well can have this confidence if you humble yourself, repent of your sins, and call on Jesus as Lord and Savior of your life.

How Do I Choose a Church?
Is My Church Leading
Me Astray?

AFTER SPENDING A lot of time reading and studying Paul's letters, It has become more and more apparent to me that many churches around the world are guilty of preaching a different gospel than the one in the Bible that was originally proclaimed by the early church fathers.

Before I go any further, I want to be clear that I am in no way condemning any one church or individual because of religious affiliation. I personally think that there are people in every Protestant and Catholic Church who will be saved, but I am equally convinced that there are people in every Protestant and Catholic Church who will not be saved. It is not my place or desire to judge. Each individual's salvation is between them and God. God knows each person's heart even better than we know it ourselves. My aim is to present the information I have gleaned from Scripture in a loving way and, Lord willing, leave you in a better position from which to evaluate your own spiritual security. Because of differing doctrinal statements and viewpoints among churches and denominations, the possibility exists that some churches are not teaching a doctrine that will lead to a saving knowledge and understanding of God's grace and salvation. While this admonition and any subsequent dialog may be unnecessary, the last thing that I want is to get to heaven and find that I had not said enough, and that friends and loved ones are suffering for eternity.

A major theme in the Apostle Paul's letters in the New Testament is whether we are saved by faith alone or by works of the Law. Paul asserts in Galatians, Ephesians, and Romans, that salvation and justification before God is by faith alone, apart from works of the Law.

> Yet we know that a person is not justified by works of the Law but through faith in Jesus Christ, so we also have believed in Christ Jesus, in order to be justified by faith in Christ and not by works of the Law, because by works of the Law no one will be justified. (Galatians 2:16)

> For by grace you have been saved through faith. And this is not your own doing; it is the gift of God, not a result of works, so that no one may boast. (Ephesians 2:8–9)

> Then what becomes of our boasting? It is excluded. By what kind of Law? By a Law of works? No, but by the Law of faith. For we hold that one is justified by faith apart from works of the Law. (Romans 3:27–28)

A common argument to the contrary is based on a passage in James. In this passage, James demonstrates that salvation requires works in order to be complete.

> You see that a person is justified by works and not by faith alone. (James 2:24)

This argument fails with the assumption that both Paul and James are addressing the same thing. If indeed they are talking about the same thing, this contradictory teaching poses a problem for the Scripture of a sovereign God. This is something a sovereign, omniscient God would never allow. The difference between the teachings of Paul and James is the object before which we are justified. Paul speaks of justification before God, which is by faith alone. James demonstrates that once we are saved by faith, we are justified before men as saved only when our works demonstrate our faith. As far as the world is concerned, our faith is useless if there is no visible, associated action accompanying our faith. But that does not mean that an individual professing faith is not justified before God and thus not saved. If an individual sincerely professes faith in the saving grace of our Lord Jesus Christ, that individual is at that moment justified before God and has eternal life. Once God begins the sanctifying work in someone's life, He will carry it through to completion. Each individual's development is at different levels, however, and the outward manifestation of the faith of someone progressing at a slower rate of change than others may not be as readily apparent in the eyes of the world as someone else who is further along, or more rapidly advancing in his or her spiritual development.

While a faith decision and justification before God is instantaneous, the sincerity of one's faith conversion will only be evidenced over time. If there is no increase of any kind in the fruit generated through an individual's faith, and no change in the life of a person over time, it may, but not necessarily, indicate that the individual in question was not truly sincere in his or her profession, and therefore never saved. It may also mean that an individual was saved, but God's work in his or her life has not yet been made manifest. For anyone truly saved, they can never lose their salvation. Paul explains it beautifully in Galatians 4, showing that a believing faith brings us into a relationship with God, in which we are adopted as His children, this being a permanent transaction not dependent on any action on our part. Jesus' words in the gospel of John give us peace about the security of our salvation in Christ Jesus.

> "I give them eternal life, and they will never perish, and no one will snatch them out of my hand. My Father, who has given them to me, is greater than all, and no one is able to snatch them out

of the Father's hand. I and the Father are one."
(John 10:28–30)

This assumption also requires that we are clear about each author's definition of works. When Paul talks of salvation not being by works, he is speaking about works for the purpose of salvation. The works James is talking about are works of love toward fellow man, flowing from a heart devoted to God. Paul also instructs believers to make love for others a priority, and describes the fruit of the Spirit that will manifest itself in a true Spirit-led believer.

> For you were called to freedom, brothers. Only do not use your freedom as an opportunity for the flesh, but through love serve one another. For the whole Law is fulfilled in one word: "You shall love your neighbor as yourself." (Galatians 5:13–14)

> But the fruit of the Spirit is love, joy, peace, patience, kindness, goodness, faithfulness, gentleness, self-control; against such things there is no law. (Galatians 5:22–23)

Paul elaborates on how worthless our works really are in his letter to the Philippians. He describes himself as formerly being among the foremost of legalistic followers of religious practice, but considers the honors of that way of life rubbish compared to knowing Christ. He reiterates how the prophet Isaiah describes our human efforts to attain righteousness.

> Finally, my brothers, rejoice in the Lord. To write the same things to you is no trouble to me and is safe for you. Look out for the dogs, look out for the evildoers, look out for those who mutilate the flesh. For we are the real circumcision, who worship by the Spirit of God and glory in

> Christ Jesus and put no confidence in the flesh—
> though I myself have reason for confidence in the
> flesh also. If anyone else thinks he has reason for
> confidence in the flesh, I have more: circumcised
> on the eighth day, of the people of Israel, of the
> tribe of Benjamin, a Hebrew of Hebrews; as to
> the law, a Pharisee; as to zeal, a persecutor of the
> church; as to righteousness, under the law blame-
> less. But whatever gain I had, I counted as loss for
> the sake of Christ. Indeed, I count everything as
> loss because of the surpassing worth of knowing
> Christ Jesus my Lord. For his sake I have suffered
> the loss of all things and count them as rubbish,
> in order that I may gain Christ. (Philippians
> 3:1–8)

> We have all become like one who is unclean, and
> all our righteous deeds are like a polluted gar-
> ment. (Isaiah 64:6)

While I realize that my understanding of Catholicism and many mainline Protestant denominations may be limited, the doctrinal beliefs of many churches today appear to be a combination of biblical interpretation and historical tradition, rather than merely relying on the teachings in Scripture. The resulting problem is that at least some, and possibly a great deal, of the tradition-based practice is only loosely based on, and in some cases, contrary to biblical truth. Within Catholicism, for instance, salvation was defined at the Council of Trent as stemming from a combination of faith and works. This definition, however, was based more on personal convenience, feelings, and man-made wisdom than on what the Bible actually teaches. This is illustrated in the above referenced passages and others throughout Scripture. Martin Luther, after spending time reflecting on God's Word, recognized that practices in the Catholic faith were inconsistent with Scripture. Recognition of Luther's position by the Council would have been an affront to the position and authority of Catholic Church leaders. The resulting decision called for a formal proclamation from the Catholic Church contradicting Luther's position. I am unaware of any actual scriptural support for the decision and proclamation that was made at that time. In that moment, the church rejected the teaching of Scripture for man-made wisdom. There are many similar issues that are a part of Catholic and Protestant traditions and practices that were not accepted and taught by the early church, that have no scriptural support, and are counterbiblical.

If it is indeed true that the Council and subsequent Catholic leadership did not have biblical support for practical decisions being made for the church, is the gospel being preached in the Catholic Church today the same Gospel preached by Paul and the other apostles? And while the Council of Trent is specific to Catholicism, there are similar historical constructs that plague certain Protestant denominations as well. The background for church doctrine is of vital importance to the authenticity of the Gospel message that is preached. Paul addresses this adamantly in his letter to the Galatians.

> I am astonished that you are so quickly deserting him who called you in the grace of Christ and are turning to a different gospel—not that there is another one, but there are some who trouble you and want to distort the gospel of Christ. But even if we or an angel from Heaven should preach to you a gospel contrary to the one we preached to you, let him be accursed. As we have said before, so now I say again: If anyone is preaching to you a gospel contrary to the one you received, let him be accursed. (Galatians 1:6–9)

Paul's letter to the Galatians addresses an issue that was causing division in the Galatians' churches. False believers were teaching that circumcision was required for salvation. Paul countered these assertions with his explanation that salvation is by faith alone and not by works of the Law. Furthermore, he asserts that undertaking any part of the Law in an effort to assure or assist in one's salvation not only nullifies the grace of God, but places the whole weight of the Law and its fulfillment on the individual. This is what Jesus willingly took upon Himself, living His life under the Law in order to fulfill the Law. This is something only He could do, as only God could successfully live under the Law without sin. Any sin on the part of Jesus would have condemned Him under the Law, just as we all are condemned apart from the salvation that is made possible by the death and resurrection of Jesus on the cross.

> For through the Law I died to the Law, so that I might live to God. I have been crucified with Christ. It is no longer I who live, but Christ who lives in me. And the life I now live in the flesh I live by faith in the Son of God, who loved me and gave himself for me. I do not nullify the grace of God, for if justification were through the Law, then Christ died for no purpose. (Galatians 2:19–21)

> For all who rely on works of the law are under a curse; for it is written, "Cursed be everyone who does not abide by all things written in the Book of the Law, and do them." (Galatians 3:10)

> For freedom Christ has set us free; stand firm therefore, and do not submit again to a yoke of slavery. Look: I, Paul, say to you that if you accept circumcision, Christ will be of no advantage to you. I testify again to every man who accepts circumcision that he is obligated to keep the whole Law. You are severed from Christ, you who would be justified by the Law; you have fallen away from grace. For through the Spirit, by faith, we ourselves eagerly wait for the hope of righteousness. For in Christ Jesus neither circum-

> cision nor uncircumcision counts for anything, but only faith working through love. (Galatians 5:1–6)
>
> But far be it from me to boast except in the cross of our Lord Jesus Christ, by which the world has been crucified to me, and I to the world. For neither circumcision counts for anything, nor uncircumcision, but a new creation. And as for all who walk by this rule, peace and mercy be upon them, and upon the Israel of God. (Galatians 6:14–16)

Paul asserts that to accept circumcision as a part of salvation obligates one to keep the whole Law. Anyone who accepts circumcision, or any part of the Law, is under a curse because it is impossible for anyone other than Jesus to keep the whole Law. It is not even enough to say at a turning point in our lives, when we realize our need for perfection, that we will live "from this point on in perfection." By that point in our lives, we have already been separated from God by a sinful nature, evidenced through countless acts of defiance and self-will. Anyone who has children knows, without a doubt, that by the time a child is old enough to truly recognize their depravity before a Holy God, it is already too late. And, while I know this is absolutely absurd and impossible aside from God Himself, if someone did somehow manage to make it through childhood without ever sinning, if they then have children of their own, they will never make it through adulthood free of sin. Sin has left us under a curse that afflicts every human being ever born of the seed of Adam. The effect of this curse is death, because any sin separates us from God, the source of life.

But even if it were possible for someone other than Jesus to keep the whole law, which it's not, providing a standard for which we can earn our salvation was not the purpose for the Law. The Law was intended to reveal the holiness of God and our unworthiness before a Holy God. No one could ever expect to meet the requirements of the Law, leaving us completely deserving of the wrath of God that is poured out against all sin. The Jews viewed the Law as a standard of conduct, which could lead to salvation and took it to ridiculous ends. But they failed to understand the Law's true purpose of leading us to Christ. An individual cannot, by one's own designs, attain salvation, because by pursuing one's own designs, that person is pursuing a man-based salvation. When our focus is on ourselves, we are not depending on God. As Paul points out in Galatians 3, the Law is a teacher, leading us to Christ by showing us that we cannot in any way accomplish perfection through our own efforts.

> For if the inheritance comes by the law, it no longer comes by promise; but God gave it to Abraham by a promise. Why then the law? It was added because of transgressions, until the offspring should come to whom the promise had been made, and it was put in place through angels by an intermediary. Now an intermediary implies more than one, but God is one. Is the law then contrary to the promises of God? Certainly not! For if a law had been given that could give life, then righteousness would indeed be by the law. But the Scripture imprisoned everything under sin, so that the promise by faith in Jesus Christ might be given to those who believe. Now before faith came, we were held captive under the law, imprisoned until the coming faith would be revealed. So then, the law was our guardian until Christ came, in order that we might be justified by faith. But now that faith has come, we are no longer under a guardian, for in Christ Jesus you are all sons of God, through faith. (Galatians 3:18–26)

For the Galatians, the issue was circumcision, but the Law is much more comprehensive than merely circumcision. At the end of his letter, Paul issues a blessing that this example should be used as a rule. Salvation is by faith alone, apart from works. Anyone, then, who adds works of any kind as means or assurance of salvation, or in any other way accepts any part in salvation as coming from his or her self, is severed from Christ and fallen away from grace.

While salvation is accessible to any individual in any church, and while I am not in any position to judge whether or not any individual is saved, I urge you to examine your own salvation to know whether you are building your faith on the solid foundation of Jesus, or in any way on your own actions. Is there any practicing instruction of works that your church has directed that you must follow for you to receive eternal life? Or do you believe your salvation is in any way based on how much good you have done? If your answer is no, that is great, and I am happy to know that we will together enjoy an eternity with God. If your answer to that question is yes, however, you may not be in a saving relationship with Jesus. Jesus' saving work was complete with His death and resurrection. Adding works is equivalent to rejecting the sufficiency of Jesus' work on the cross and trying to find your own way.

In Jesus' words, He confirms that He did not come to destroy the Law, but to fulfill it, so that in Him and Him alone can we be saved.

> "Do not think that I have come to abolish the Law or the Prophets; I have not come to abolish them but to fulfill them." (Matthew 5:17)

> Jesus said to him, "I am the way, and the truth, and the life. No one comes to the Father except through me." (John 14:6)

This is great news. Because it does not in any way depend on what we do, it is possible to know for sure that we are saved. We can take comfort in knowing that if our conversion and salvation is genuine, there is nothing we can ever do that will remove us from God's grace.

> For all have sinned and fall short of the glory
> of God, and are justified by his grace as a gift,
> through the redemption that is in Christ Jesus.
> (Romans 3:23–24)

> For the wages of sin is death, but the free gift
> of God is eternal life in Christ Jesus our Lord.
> (Romans 6:23)

These two passages speak of salvation as a gift, and not only that, but a free gift. We need to do nothing to accept it, but faithfully believe.

> If you confess with your mouth that Jesus is
> Lord and believe in your heart that God raised
> him from the dead, you will be saved. For with
> the heart one believes and is justified, and with
> the mouth one confesses and is saved. (Romans
> 10:9–10)

If you think that you may possibly not be saved because you have been trying to "help your salvation through religious practice or good works," or have never at a specific moment prayed to God and accepted His gift, all you need to do is pray. Humble yourself before God, confess your sinful nature to Him, and admit to Him that you are a sinner and cannot by any means do anything to assist in your own salvation. Thank Jesus for taking your sin on Himself and accepting the penalty that you deserve. Accept His free gift of salvation and eternal life by asking Him to come into your life as Lord and Savior.

If you have come to the conclusion that you had already been saved, or prayed to God and accepted His gift of salvation today, congratulations and welcome to the family of God. I am not saying that you necessarily have to change churches or do anything differently if what you are doing in worship and practice is merely an expression of your love for God and others. If, on the other hand, you are relying on church rules and traditions for salvation, or if you recognize teachings that do not have biblical support, you would be wise to consider looking elsewhere. Connect yourself with a church that is founded on and teaches the Bible as the only reliable source of information about God, who is the utmost authority in our lives. There can and will be no further revelation coming from God through the church, the pope, your pastor, or anything else that contradicts what God has already given us in His Word. If something contradicts God's Word, it is not from God and must be rejected. Do not allow the comfort of familiarity with current conditions to keep you in a church that is ultimately detrimental to your spiritual growth and development.

> But now that you have come to know God, or rather to be known by God, how can you turn back again to the weak and worthless elementary principles of the world, whose slaves you want to be once more? You observe days and months and seasons and years! I am afraid I may have labored over you in vain. (Galatians 4:9–11)
>
> For freedom Christ has set us free; stand firm therefore, and do not submit again to a yoke of slavery. (Galatians 5:1)

It is vitally important for the church you attend to be firmly grounded in God's Word, especially in core doctrines. It is important that you are in a place where you can glorify God and grow in your relationship with Him.

It is also important that the primary goal of your church be the spread of the Gospel message of salvation through Christ and Christ alone, the motivation and objective that drove the early church fathers. Your church may be excellent in social justice, providing for the poor and downtrodden, and that is good, but if it has veered away from the Great Commission of presenting the means to salvation, it is misguided and no different than any other man-made institution seeking to make this world a better place in which to live.

The early church saw the importance of caring for community needs and designated elders to manage these affairs. But the message of salvation was of utmost importance. Making the lives of those in difficult conditions better in the present is a worthy goal, but if they are destined for eternal torment, the temporary benefit they receive now is of little worth. The church you attend should have this balance as well.

Finally, don't take my word on this. Pray and ask God to guide you and direct your understanding as you read His Word for yourself. Do not take for granted that everything you hear from the pulpit is true, but get into God's Word yourself and test what you hear against what God has stated directly in His Word. God will never contradict or change what He has previously revealed to us. It may be that over time we gain a new understanding of passages of Scripture, but this understanding will always be in agreement within the whole context of God's written Word. The more time you spend in God's Word, the more you will grow and develop a personal relationship with Jesus. The deeper and more intimate your relationship becomes, the more certain you will be of your salvation. The more confident you are of your salvation, the easier it will be for you to live with eternity in view.

CPSIA information can be obtained
at www.ICGtesting.com
Printed in the USA
BVHW090103281119
564987BV00004B/9/P